Robots In The Classroom

John Blankenship
Samuel Mishal

First Edition
September 2009

Contents At A Glance

Table Of Contents

Preface

Most introductory programming classes today bore the student with examples and exercises that are inappropriate for anyone new to programming. In most cases, the examples and applications studied are far from exciting because they don't address real-world situations. Instead, students are shown how to count the number of words in a sentence or find the factorial of a number. While such projects can teach useful techniques, they are hardly subjects that will excite someone new to programming.

Unfortunately, even when teachers try to introduce something exciting in the classroom, they often find many obstacles. Most modern languages, for example, require the student to learn about classes or components, as well as a cryptic syntax, before *anything* (let alone something meaningful) can be accomplished. This means that most students fail to grasp even basic programming concepts because they are too busy trying to cope with the idiosyncrasies of the language itself.

RobotBASIC addresses all of these problems. It is a powerful, yet extremely easy-to-use language that is available for any Window's based PC. In addition to all the commands you expect in a computer language, it has many features that make it easy to create interesting and motivational applications even for people new to programming. We are convinced of its potential as an educational tool and want to make it available to everyone. You can download your free copy from:

www.RobotBASIC.com

This book will use RobotBASIC to teach you about programming while you explore simple robotic applications. You will learn how to manually control a mobile robot and how to give it enough intelligence to make some decisions on its own. Once you've learned the basics of mobile robotics, you'll be introduced to robotic arms and walking robots.

Usually, when these subjects are studied, you need thousands of dollars of equipment that has to be shared among all the participants in a class. In this book, however, all of the robots will be provided through computer simulations. Besides eliminating the costs and hassles associated with purchasing and maintaining real robots, the simulations allow every student in the class to have his or her own robot for use at school and at home.

No previous knowledge of programming is required. This book will gradually give you everything you need before progressing to more complex topics. This does not mean that you won't have to study. Programming requires logical thinking and problem-solving skills that take time and practice to develop and you should complete the suggested exercises to obtain the maximum benefit from this text.

Students at almost any grade level can use the early portions of the book. As the book progresses though, the projects become harder and are more suitable for high school or even college level classes.

Fortunately, while learning how to program with this book you will have fun exploring interesting ideas and relevant applications.

Chapter 1

What is a Program?

Before we start programming a robot, we must learn some basic principles of programming. A program is simply a set of instructions that allows you to tell a computer what to do. It is not unlike the instructions you would create to tell a person what to do.

Suppose you wanted to tell a person how to get to your house. You would give them a step-by-step set of instructions explaining what to do first, what to do next, and so on. A simple computer program is the same.

1.1 Computer Languages

You can write the instructions on how to go to your house in any language. You might use French or German, for example, instead of English. If you want people to be able to follow the directions you must use a language they understand. The same applies for a computer program.

The internal design of a computer dictates the languages that it can understand. Simple computers, such as the type found in microwave ovens, generally have to be told what to do using cryptic and obscure languages that resemble shorthand. This is necessary because small computers often have limited power and minimal memory.

Today's typical PC, on the other hand, has a huge amount of memory and thousands of times the power of the computers used to put the first men on the moon. Because of this versatility, there have been many languages written for the PC. This book will use a language called RobotBASIC.

1.2 RobotBASIC

RobotBASIC is a very powerful language, yet easy to learn. It has all the mathematical capabilities you would expect from any computer language, and even a few seldom found in other systems. It even has an integrated robot simulator that makes it easy to learn how to program a mobile robot. It also has a wide range of powerful graphic commands that make it easy to create additional simulations, such as a walking robot or a robotic arm.

One of the best things about RobotBASIC is that it is very easy to use. Another advantage is that it is totally free. RobotBASIC is a language that is powerful enough to handle complex problems and yet easy to learn and fun to use. You can download your FREE copy of RobotBASIC by visiting the web site:

www.RobotBASIC.com

> **Note:** We suggest you download the ZIP file created especially for this book. There are other zip files with many demo programs and files for other books. After you learn the fundamentals about programming with RobotBASIC from this book, you can download some of the other zip files and study all the example programs provided in them.
>
> **Note:** The web site provides information for installing everything on your computer so you will be ready to start creating programs.

When you first run RobotBASIC, you will see a screen similar to the one shown in Figure 1.1. View and accept the license agreement, which basically says that you can freely use the program and give it to your friends, but you cannot sell it.

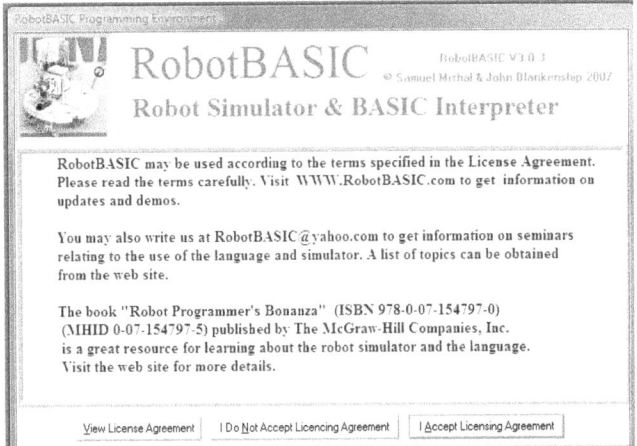

Figure 1.1: This is the opening screen for RobotBASIC

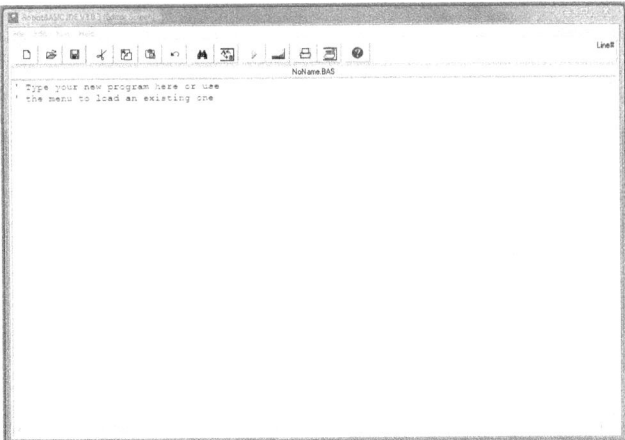

Figure 1.2: When you see this screen you are ready to program.

Upon accepting the license, you will see the screen shown in Figure 1.2 with some highlighted *comments* that show where you will type the programs you write. Since these comments are highlighted, the first key you type will replace them. They can also be erased using the **BACKSPACE** key if you wish.

1.3 The Output or Terminal Screen

The output screen for RobotBASIC is composed of tiny dots called pixels. RobotBASIC allows you to create graphics on this screen by changing the colors of these pixels. In order to write graphics programs, you need to know how pixels are organized.

The size of the screen is 800 pixels wide and 600 pixels tall. The pixels are numbered both horizontally and vertically starting with the number zero. Each pixel is defined by two numbers called *coordinates* that specify its position on the screen. The first number specifies the horizontal position (often referred to as the X-coordinate) and the second specifies the vertical position (the Y-coordinate).

A pixel at position 100,200 for example, would be positioned 100 pixels from the left side of the screen and 200 pixels down from the top. The pixel at position 0,0 is at the upper left corner of the screen while the coordinates 799,599 refer to the bottom right corner.

1.4 Drawing Lines

RobotBASIC allows you to draw a line on the screen using the Line command, which requires you to specify the starting and ending coordinates. The example below will draw a line from the upper-left corner of the screen to the lower-right corner. Notice how the coordinates 0,0 and 799,599 are entered.

```
Line 0,0,799,599
```

1.5 Running Programs

In order to see the line actually draw on the screen, we must tell RobotBASIC to run the program. We can do that in several ways. The easiest way is by clicking the 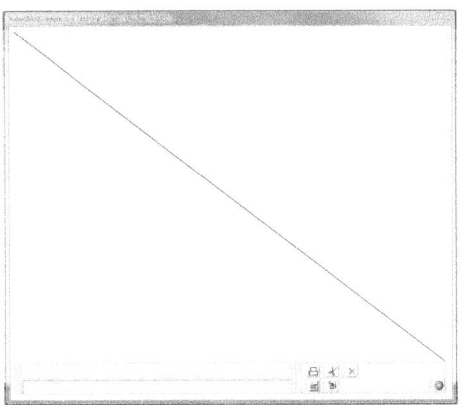 button (the green triangle) at the top of the screen. You could also use the mouse and click the RUN menu item at the top of the screen and then click the first option (Run Program). If you look carefully at that menu item, you will see it gives you a short cut option (*Ctrl-R*). This means you can also run a program by holding down the *Ctrl* key and pressing the letter R (or r).

Many actions in RobotBASIC can be achieved in a variety of ways. In the future, we will only point out one easy method for doing things. Refer to RobotBASIC's help files (by clicking the button at the top of the editor screen) to get further information.

If you enter and run the one-line program just discussed, you will get the screen shown in Figure 1.3. Notice the line is drawn from the upper-left corner (coordinates 0,0) to the lower-right corner (coordinates 799,599).

Figure 1.3: A line drawn between two corners.

Now that you know how to enter and run a program, let's create something slightly more interesting. Click the in the top right corner of the output (terminal) screen to close it (returning you to the editor screen), and then type in the lines shown in Figure 1.4 (notice our original line is included in the new program. Notice how some letters have been capitalized to make reading easier. The capitalization in this example program is not required, but it is recommended.

```
SetColor RED
LineWidth 3
Line 0,0,799,599
SetColor Green
LineWidth 20
Line 799,0,100,500
End
```

Figure 1.4: This program draws two colorful lines.

Let's examine the program in Figure 1.4. Each line is executed in turn starting at the beginning and continuing to the last line. The first line sets the color used for drawing to RED. The next line establishes how many pixels wide the drawn lines should be. This means that the line drawn from 0,0 to 799,599 will be red and 3 pixels wide.

The next two lines in the program set the color to green and the width to 10. Notice that these actions only affect future lines to be drawn not any lines that have already been drawn. This means the next line in the program draws a wide green line from the upper-right corner of the screen (799,0) to a position near the lower-left corner. The end point (100,500) is positioned 100 pixels from the left and 500 pixels from the top. Run the program to see the results.

Notice the last line in the program is an END statement. It tells the program to quit. In this particular case, the program will stop even if you did not have an END because there are no more lines to execute. If you add lines after the END statement, they will not execute.

1.6 Saving and Retrieving Programs

You can save your programs at any time by pressing the Save 🖫 button. This allows you retrieve the program later using the Open 🖙 button. You should develop the habit of saving your programs often and definitely before you run them. This will ensure that you do not lose all your hard work if the computer crashes for some reason.

1.7 Errors in a Program

If you make a typing mistake in a program the computer will not be able to understand what you want it to do. When you run a program that has errors, RobotBASIC will alert you with an error message. If in the fifth line of Figure 1.4, for example, you wrongly spell LineWidth as LinWidth then running the program will create the error shown in Figure 1.5.

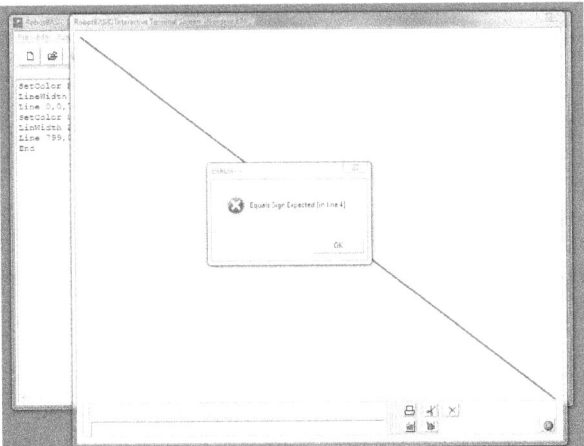

Figure 1.5: RobotBASIC tells you when it finds an error.

Notice that the program drew the red line, since the error did not occur until after that point in the program. The error message in this case (**Equals Sign Expected**) will mean more to you later in the book. At this point, all your errors are most likely caused by simple typos.

Notice that the message also tells you that the error is in Line 4 (and not Line 5 as you might expect). This is because RobotBASIC starts numbering program lines with Line 0. If you press the *OK* button, you will be returned to the editor screen and the line containing the error will be highlighted to help you locate the problem. As we proceed through the book, we will examine errors and how to find them in more detail.

1.8 Adding to the Program

Suppose we want to draw a line from the center of the screen horizontally to the right edge of the screen. The center of the screen should be at 400,300 because the entire screen is 800 wide and 600 tall. If we want the ending point to be the right edge of the screen, then the X-coordinate should be 799 and the Y-coordinate needs to be the same as the Y-coordinate for the starting point, or 300 (to ensure that the line is horizontal). Add the following line just before the END statement in Figure 1.4 and run the program again. Can you predict what color the line will be? Can you change the line so it is 5 pixels wide and BLUE?

```
Line 400,300,799,300
```

☑ **Note:** For more colors, refer to the CONSTANTS page of the help files.

1.9 Connecting Lines (the easy way)

In addition to the Line command, RobotBASIC also has the LineTo command which requires only one set of coordinates, and draws a line to that point from the last point plotted. The lines below, for example, will draw a triangle. The first line draws one side. The second line continues drawing to a new point and finally, the last line draws back to the beginning point. Create a program with these lines and verify that it draws a triangle.

```
Line 200,200,300,200
LineTo 300,400
LineTo 200,200
```

Before we move on, let's test your knowledge of the material covered so far. Your goal is to write a program that will draw the triangle and the rectangle shown in Figure 1.6. The figure shows the distances (in pixels) to various sides and points of the objects. Try to write a program to draw these shapes before looking at the answer in Appendix A.

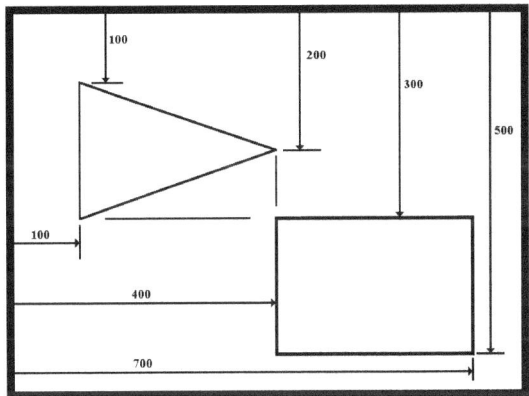

Figure 1.6: Use this information to determine the coordinates of each point of the objects.

1.10 The Robot Simulator

Now that you know about screen coordinates, let's see how we can create a robot and move it around the screen. The robot simulator in RobotBASIC creates a robot using the rLocate command. The following line will create a robot at coordinates 100,200.

```
rLocate 100,200
```

Enter the above line as a single line program and run it. You will see a screen with a small circular robot in the upper-left corner. The line inside the circle indicates the direction the robot is facing (the default direction is up).

Enter the program shown in Figure 1.7. It demonstrates how to create a robot, tell it to turn right 90° and then move forward 500 pixels, turn around, and go back to its original position. Run the program and verify that it does what is expected.

```
rLocate 100,200
rTurn 90
rForward 500
rTurn 180
rForward 500
End
```

Figure 1.7: This program moves a robot on the screen.

There are several things to notice in Figure 1.7. All the commands that relate directly to the robot in RobotBASIC start with the letter 'r'. Notice also that some letters in commands are capitalized. This is only done for readability. The commands in RobotBASIC are *not* case-sensitive.

The rForward command moves the robot forward a specified number of pixels (or backwards if you use a negative number for the distance to be moved). The rTurn command turns the robot clockwise the specified number of degrees (or counter-clockwise if the value is negative).

If the robot moves too fast on your computer you can slow it down by inserting the following line immediately after the rLocate command.

```
rSpeed 10
```

The *parameter* (a value given to a command , 10 in this example) in the rSpeed command determines how fast the robot moves. The larger the number the slower the movement, the default number 0 produces the fastest speed.

In some situations it may be an advantage to slow down the robot in order to be able to observe its actions, but usually we will want the robot to move as fast as it can. Try adding two rSpeed commands to Figure 1.6 to cause the robot to move from left to right slowly, but then move quickly as it travels back to its original position. If you have trouble, refer to the answers in Appendix A.

1.11 Summary

In this chapter, you have learned:

- ❏ About the coordinate system used by RobotBASIC.
- ❏ How to enter and run a RobotBASIC program.
- ❏ How to draw shapes using lines of different colors and different widths.
- ❏ How to create and move the simulated robot at different speeds.

1.12 Exercises

Before moving on to the next chapter, test your knowledge and skill by trying the following exercises. Give each problem your best effort before reviewing the answers given in Appendix A.

1. Create a robot at the upper-left corner of the screen and make the robot move around the perimeter of the screen (in a rectangular motion) until it goes back to its original position.

> ✍ **Note:** If you move the robot so that it hits a wall, it will cause an error. This situation will be addressed in a later chapter.

2. Create a robot at the upper-left corner of the screen and make the robot move diagonally down to the

lower-right corner and then back to its original position.

> ☑ **Note:** The RobotBASIC ZIP file you downloaded contains some of the larger programs in this book already typed for you. In most cases though, you will have to type the programs yourself - don't worry, most are short. Forcing you to type the programs is intentional. We have taught programming to many students, and we know you will learn more and learn faster if you become fully involved with the programming process. Trust us! The results will be worth the extra efforts you are about to face.

Chapter 2

Variables

In the previous chapter you were introduced to programming. In this chapter you will learn about variables and how they help in writing more sophisticated programs.

2.1 What is a Variable?

A variable is an area in the memory of the computer that is given a name. This area can store a number (or text) whose value can be changed during the progress of a program. This is why it is called a variable. If you have studied Algebra you know that you can use variables in formulas to do calculations. Computer programs can do the same thing with programming variables.

For example, if we are talking about a rectangle it might have a width of 200 and a height of 100, but these numbers refer to one specific rectangle. Often in programming, we would like to write *code* (programming statements) that refers to a generalized situation. For example, we might want our program to draw rectangles and refer to the size of the rectangle using the variables called **width** and **height**.

2.2 Case Sensitivity

Unlike commands, the variables in RobotBASIC *are* case sensitive. This means that **width**, **Width**, and **WIDTH** are all *different* variables. This can be advantageous, but it also means you must be careful not to make typographical errors.

Variables are often meaningful words (like **width**) but they can also be just a single letter (like **A** or **x**). Variables in RobotBASIC can hold numbers (like 6 and 92.3) and words (like "hello"). For now, we will only be using numbers. We assign values to a variable using the = sign. We can also perform calculations using variables. Figure 2.1 shows a program to help clarify these ideas.

```
cat = 6
dog = 4
bird = cat*3 + dog
print cat
cat = cat * dog
Print cat
Print dog
Print bird
End
```

Figure 2.1: This program demonstrates variables.

If you run the program in Figure 2.1, it will print four numbers (6, 24, 4, and 22). Let's see how that happens. When the program starts, the variable **cat** is assigned a value of 6 and **dog** is assigned 4.

In the next line, **cat** is multiplied by 3 (forming 18) and added to **dog** (forming 22), which is stored in the variable **bird**. The next line multiplies the current value of **cat** (6) and **dog** to form 24. That value is stored back into **cat** (overwriting the previous value of 6).

The `Print` statements print the values of the variables specified as parameters. Notice that **cat** is printed twice so you can see that its value changes. The first `Print` statement will print at the top of the screen and each subsequent `Print` will print on the next line down. There are other options for `Print` as well as other commands for printing. We will discuss other options when they are needed, or you can refer to the RobotBASIC HELP file for more information.

> ✎ **Note:** RobotBASIC will issue an error if you try to use a variable as part of a calculation before you have assigned it a value.

2.3 Rectangles

Let's try an example that demonstrates the graphics command, `rectangle`. You have to give it four *parameters*. The first two represent the coordinates of the upper-left corner and the last two, the lower-right corner of the rectangle to be drawn. As an example, the line of code below will draw a rectangle whose upper-left corner is 50,100 and the lower-right corner is 500,250. Notice the width of this rectangle is 450 and its height is 150 (the width is the difference between the two X-coordinates and the height is the difference between the two Y-coordinates).

```
Rectangle 50, 100, 500, 250
```

The program in Figure 2.2 will draw four rectangles on the screen as shown in Figure 2.3.

```
LineWidth 3
Rectangle 100,100,350,200
Rectangle 400,100,650,200
Rectangle 400,350,650,450
Rectangle 100,350,350,450
End
```

Figure 2.2: This program draws four rectangles.

Study the code of Figure 2.2 carefully and make sure you see how the rectangles are formed. Notice that the width of every rectangle is 250 and the height of every rectangle is 100. Each rectangle is drawn at a different position.

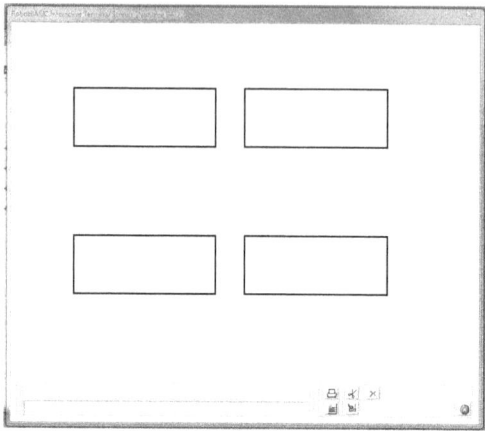

Figure 2.3: These rectangles are created by Figure 2.2.

2.4 Using Variables

For many applications, it would be better if we could specify the size and position of a rectangle (we will see why later) using the variables **x**, **y**, **width**, and **height**. If the values of these variables have already been set, we can draw the rectangle using the following line of code. Notice how the values for the lower-right coordinates are calculated by adding the width and height to the coordinates (x,y) of the upper-left corner.

```
Rectangle x, y, x+width, y+height
```

The use of variables and *expressions* (calculation formulas) as part of the parameters makes it easier to specify how rectangles are positioned and drawn. If we wanted to draw the four rectangles shown in Figure 2.3 using our new methodology we could use the program in Figure 2.4.

Study the program carefully. Notice how variables are used to control where and how the rectangles are drawn. Let's look at a situation that takes advantage of using variables.

```
LineWidth 3
width = 250
height = 100
x = 100
y = 100
Rectangle x,y,x+width,y+height
x = 400
Rectangle x,y,x+width,y+height
y = 350
Rectangle x,y,x+width,y+height
x = 100
Rectangle x,y,x+width,y+height
End
```

Figure 2.4: This program also draws four Rectangles.

Let's assume you had written the program in Figure 2.4 and then decided that you wanted the rectangles to be squares. We could make this happen for *all* the rectangles by changing only the second line to set the width to 100. Make that change and run the program again. Each of the rectangles should now be a square.

Now let's assume you want to do the same thing with the program in Figure 2.2. Enter this program and make sure it is working properly. Then, change it so that it draws four squares instead of four rectangles. Don't take this assignment lightly. Please take the time to do it. You will be very surprised at how much effort it takes to make the changes when compared to the single change needed for Figure 2.4. As we proceed thorough the book, you will see more and more examples of how variables make programming easier. In fact, let's look at one more example right now.

2.5 User Input

We want to use the program shown in Figure 2.4, but instead of having a prefixed height and width we want the user of the program to be able to specify the height and width of the rectangles. The program in Figure 2.5 shows how this can be accomplished. Most of the program is exactly the same as in Figure 2.4.

Let's look at some of the new items in the program. The first two `Print` statements are different. Instead of printing the value of a variable, they are given a parameter that is enclosed in quotes. When this is done, the `Print` command prints the information between the quotes as is.

The next two lines introduce the `Input` command. When `Input` is executed, the user is prompted to enter a value inside the input box at the bottom of the terminal screen. The value entered will be stored in the variable specified. In order to tell the user what to do, the text included between the quotes (in the `Input` statements) is displayed just above the input box. Enter the program shown in Figure 2.5 and run it to see how the `Input` command works.

When you run the program, you will see the items displayed by the first two `Print` statements. You will also see the phrase "Enter Width" displayed near the bottom of the screen above the input box. Type a value (e.g. 100) in the box and press the **ENTER** key.

```
Print "This program will draw four rectangles."
Print "It will allow you to specify width and height."
Input "Enter Width", width
Input "Enter Height", height
x = 100
y = 100
Rectangle x,y,x+width,y+height
x = 400
Rectangle x,y,x+width,y+height
y = 350
Rectangle x,y,x+width,y+height
x = 100
Rectangle x,y,x+width,y+height
End
```

Figure 2.5: This program lets the user specify the height and width of the rectangles to be drawn.

You will immediately see a new prompt asking you to enter the height. Again enter the number 100. You will then see four rectangles (now squares because the height and width are both 100). Try running the program a few times and enter different values to verify you are actually controlling how the rectangles are being drawn.

2.6 Circles and Ellipses

RobotBASIC has a `Circle` command that is very much like the `Rectangle` command. The parameters for `Circle` define a rectangle just as they did with the `Rectangle` command. Instead of drawing the rectangle though, `Circle` draws a circle (or ellipse) inside the boundaries defined by the rectangle. Change any of the `Rectangle` statements in the programs used in this chapter to `Circle` and see what happens when you run them again.

2.7 Using the Robot

Now that we have the ability to draw lines, rectangles, and circles on the screen, we can create objects that would act as obstacles which our simulated robot has to avoid. Look at the code shown in Figure 2.6 which creates the screen shown in Figure 2.7.

If you understand the concepts we have covered so far, it should be easy to see how the three objects were drawn on the screen. Notice that the robot has been initialized near the center of the screen. Notice also that a *comment* line has been added to show you where you should add your code.

A comment is any line that begins with two slashes (//). Comments (everything on the line past the //) are ignored when the program is executed. They can serve as notes or reminders of why you did certain things or to state the purpose of sections of your code. We will discuss this concept in more detail later in the book.

```
LineWidth 3
Rectangle 200,400,500,550
Circle 200,200,400,300
Line 400,100,700,500
rLocate 350,350
// Enter your code here

End
```

Figure 2.6: This code creates an environment for the robot.

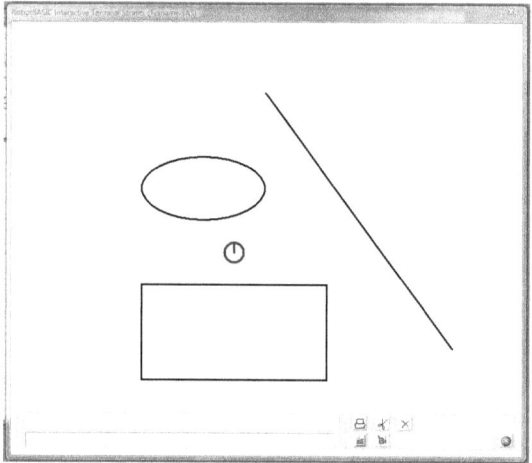

Figure 2.7: You must write code to move the robot
to the upper-right corner of the screen.

Your assignment is to use a series of rTurn and rForward
statements to move the robot through the environment with
the objective of reaching the upper-right corner of the
screen.

The robot may take any path you wish and can turn and
forward in any way you want, using as many commands as
necessary to complete the task. However, we recommend
that you enter only one or two new commands before
running the program to test your code. The reason is that
when the robot bumps into any of the objects on the screen

(or even one of the exterior walls) it will cause an error. If you get errors, examine your program and make the necessary corrections. The assignment is considered completed when the robot reaches the upper-right corner of the screen without causing an error (which means that it had successfully avoided the objects).

2.8 Summary

In this chapter you have learned:
- About variables and how they can be used.
- How to draw rectangles and circles on the terminal screen.
- How the Input command can allow the user to alter the actions of a program.
- How to move the robot through a cluttered environment.

2.9 Exercises

Before moving on to the next chapter, test your knowledge and skill by trying the following exercises. Give each problem your best effort before reviewing the answers given in Appendix A.

1. Enter the program in Figure 2.2 and verify that it runs properly. Add commands to make each of the rectangles a different color.

2. Enter the program in Figure 2.4 and verify that it runs properly. Add commands to make each of the rectangles a different line width.

3. Modify the programs in both Figures 2.2 and 2.4 so that they draw 100 by 100 pixel squares instead of rectangles.

4. Enter the program in Figure 2.5 and verify that it runs properly. Add commands to allow the user to also specify (with the INPUT command) the x,y position of the *last* rectangle drawn.

5. Enter the program in 2.6 and add your code to move the robot to the upper-right corner of the screen without causing an error.

Chapter 3

Loops

Every program we have written so far has executed the program statements in a sequential order, one line after another from beginning to end. The real power of programming though, lies in the ability to control how the execution flows through the program. In some cases we may need to repeatedly execute some lines of code or execute some lines only if certain conditions are satisfied. In this chapter we will see how *loop-structures* can be used to achieve this to help make more powerful and efficient programs.

3.1 Efficiency

Let's start our discussion by examining why loop-structures make a program more efficient. Suppose you owned a tree planting service and hired people to dig the holes to plant the trees. Also assume that you need to give your hole-diggers some instructions. Perhaps they would look something like this:

> Remove one shovel full of dirt.
> Remove one shovel full of dirt.
> Remove one shovel full of dirt.
> ......

Get the idea? The number of shovels of dirt that need to be removed depends, of course, on how big the shovel is, how full they make it, and how big a hole you need. And, who wants to take the time to write the same command dozens or even hundreds of times. Just as this does not make sense in our example of instructions for a hole-digger, it does not make sense for programming either.

3.2 The WHILE—WEND Structure

What we need is a way of telling the hole-digger (or the computer) how to dig the hole without having to say the same thing so many times. Better instructions for the hole-digger might look something like this:

```
while the hole is less than 2 feet deep
    remove one shovel of dirt
wend
```

The idea is that the actions between the while and the wend statements must be executed over and over as long as the hole has not reached a depth of two feet. The wend (while-end) at the end serves as a marker indicating the end of the while loop. Notice also that the interior of the loop is indented so that it is easier to identify that this is code that has a specific purpose or action attributed to it. The indenting is not required, but is highly recommended because it makes the code easier to read and understand.

3.3 The REPEAT—UNTIL Structure

Another way to write the above instructions might look like this:

```
repeat the following
    remove one shovel of dirt
until the hole is 2 feet deep
```

The above example essentially accomplishes the same task as before, but it uses a different approach. In this case the digging continues *until* the hole is deep enough – in the first case the digging continued as long as the whole was *not* deep enough. These may seem the same, but there are some differences.

In the second situation the digger will *always* remove at least one shovel full, even if the hole is already deep enough before he starts. This is true because the decision about whether to continue or not comes at the end of the loop.

In the first example, the decision comes at the beginning, which means if the hole is already deep enough, no dirt will be removed. In most cases, either method will work, but let's examine some situations that make it better, and sometimes even necessary, to use one particular structure rather than the other.

Suppose we were writing instructions on how to pick a ripe apple from a tree. Here are two ways, based on the previous examples.

```
while the apple is not ripe        repeat
    look at a new apple                look at a new apple
wend                               until the apple is ripe
pick the apple                     pick the apple
```

The principle behind both of the examples above is that the loop will continue looking at apples until a ripe apple is found. At that point the looping will stop and execution of the commands continues with the next line, which picks the apple currently being looked at.

In the example on the left, the initial decision makes no sense. How can you decide if an apple is ripe if you have not looked at one yet? This problem is solved in the example on the right because the instructions tell you to look at an apple before you are asked if it is ripe.

Let's look at another example. Suppose you want to eat some grapes. Look at these two methods for accomplishing that task.

```
while you are hungry          repeat
    eat a grape                   eat a grape
wend                          until you are not hungry
```

In this case, the while-structure makes more sense. In the repeat option, you *always* eat a grape even if you are not hungry.

These are simplified examples, but they should illustrate the principles. Creating a loop to cause an action to take place repeatedly (based on some condition) is a very efficient way of handling many tasks. In some cases, as we have seen, you must be careful how you construct the loop to ensure that the logic makes sense.

3.4 A Counting-Structure (FOR–NEXT)

There is a third way we could construct a loop. We might give instructions that tell the worker to count the actions and perform them a specific number of times (e.g. the hole-digger should remove exactly 32 shovels of dirt).

RobotBASIC has ways of creating all three of the above types of loops. You can use any of them to handle a given situation, but as we have seen, some situations are best handled by a particular type of loop. We will look at some examples here, but future chapters will address looping in more detail. Let's start by looking at an implementation of a counting loop.

3.5 Implementing the FOR–NEXT Structure

Previous chapters have shown how rForward and rTurn can be used to move the robot around the screen. For example, the program in Figure 3.1 will move the robot in a square. Notice, there are some new commands in this program that deserve some attention.

The program begins by initializing the robot with the rLocate command. The next line contains a new command that tells the simulated robot that RED is an invisible color. This means that objects drawn in RED will not be seen by the robot as objects. Things drawn in RED can be thought of as lines painted on the floor.

Our robot has a pen mounted at its center that can be lowered so it can draw on the floor while it is moving, or raised to stop drawing. The next line of code tells the robot to put the pen in the down position, and since we have told the robot that the color Red is an invisible color it will use that color to draw using the pen.

```
rLocate 200,300
rInvisible Red
rPen Down
rForward 100
rTurn 90
rForward 100
rTurn 90
rForward 100
rTurn 90
rForward 100
rTurn 90
end
```

Figure 3.1: This program moves the robot in a square and draws a RED line as it moves.

Type in the program shown in Figure 3.1 and run it to verify that the robot does indeed move in a square, leaving a red trail.

Notice that two lines in this program are repeated four times. Figure 3.2 shows how we can use a loop to repeat this action without writing so many lines of code.

Let's study how this new program works. The two lines that we want to repeat have been placed inside a counting loop that starts with a `for` statement and ends with a `next`. The `for` statement allows you to specify a variable (in this case **a**) that handles the counting. In this example, **a** is initialized to 1 and the loop will continue until it reaches 4. The current value of **a** increases by one every time the `next` statement executes, and then the loop starts over with the first line following the `for`. If you want proof that the variable **a** is actually incrementing, place the following line inside the for-loop (perhaps at the beginning of the loop, right after the `for`) and run the program to see the results.

```
print a
```

Notice, as mentioned earlier, that the statements inside the loop are indented to help identify the block of code that makes up the body of the loop.

```
rLocate 200,300
rInvisible Red
rPen Down
for a=1 to 4
   rForward 100
   rTurn 90
next
end
```

Figure 3.2: This program uses a loop to move the robot like Figure 3.1, but much more efficiently.

The second program is shorter than the first, but you might not think the loop is saving much work. After all, we only saved typing in four lines of code. Let's look at another example to help demonstrate how powerful loop structures can be.

Suppose, for example that we want our robot to draw a circle rather than a square. Before you can program the robot to do this, we must know how to do it yourself. Imagine yourself standing in a room. How would you walk in a circle? One answer is to walk forward just a little and then turn a little. If you repeated these actions enough time, you would move in circle and eventually return to your starting point. The program shown in Figure 3.3 shows how we can tell our robot to perform these actions.

If you run the program in Figure 3.3, you will see the robot leave a trail as shown in Figure 3.4. Notice the robot has started to create the circle, but has not moved nearly enough times. Try increasing the number 100 in the `for` statement to make the circle complete. Remember, we are turning the robot one degree each time through the loop. Can you guess what the number should be to complete the circle?

```
rLocate 200,300
rInvisible Red
rPen Down
for i=1 to 100
   rForward 2
   rTurn 1
next
end
```

Figure 3.3: This program uses a loop to move the robot in a circular motion.

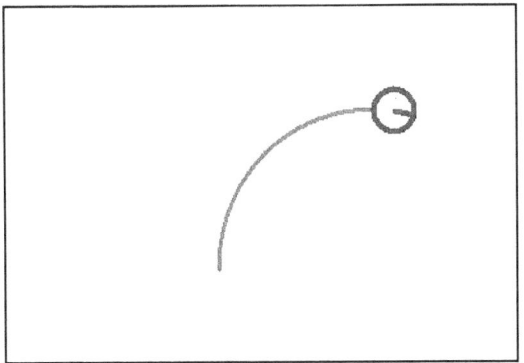

Figure 3.4: The program in Figure 3.3 will create this screen.

How would you make the robot draw the circle bigger or smaller? Try changing the values in the `rForward` and `rTurn` commands to see how the robot's behavior is affected.

3.6 Implementing a `WHILE-WEND` Loop

In order to demonstrate the while loop, we need some condition to monitor, so we will introduce the `ReadMouse` command. `ReadMouse` requires three variables as parameters. An example is shown below.

```
ReadMouse x,y,z
```

When the above line is executed, the variables **x** and **y** (you may use any variables) will be set to the current screen coordinates of the mouse cursor. The variable **z** will be set to 0 if no buttons on the mouse are pressed, 1 if the left mouse-button is pressed, and 2 if the right mouse-button is pressed.

The program in Figure 3.5 shows a simple way to use the mouse to control the robot.

```
rLocate 300,500
rSpeed 20
ReadMouse x,y,b
while b=0
  rForward 1
  ReadMouse x,y,b
wend
Print "Robot Stopped"
end
```

Figure 3.5: This program uses the mouse to stop the robot.

After the robot is initialized near the bottom of the screen, the `rSpeed` command prevents it from moving too fast for this application (adjust the parameter to make the robot move at a reasonable speed on your computer). Look now at the two actions inside the `while` loop. They will be repeated over and over as long as the variable **b** is equal to 0 (meaning no mouse buttons are pressed). Notice that there is a `ReadMouse` command *inside* the loop. If it was not inside the loop, there would be no way for the value of **b** to change and the loop would continue on forever (or until the robot hit a wall and caused an error).

Notice also that there is a `ReadMouse` before the loop too. Without this command, there would be problems, because the `while` statement would try to test the value of **b** before it has a value. Another way of solving this problem, would have been to simply set **b=0** right before the loop (instead of reading the mouse).

3.7 Implementing a `REPEAT-UNTIL` Loop

The fact that we have to initialize the value of **b** in Figure 3.5 is very important because it is another example of why sometimes one type of loop can be better than another. Look at the program in Figure 3.6.

```
rLocate 300,500
rSpeed 20
repeat
   rForward 1
   ReadMouse x,y,b
until b=1
Print "Robot Stopped"
end
```

Figure 3.6: This program also uses the mouse to stop the robot.

Notice how much more logical the `repeat-until` loop is, in this situation, than the `while-wend`. We do not have to initialize the value of **b** before the loop, because the

`ReadMouse` command inside the loop is executed *before* the `until` statement checks its value. Both programs perform the intended action, but Figure 3.6 is shorter and certainly more logical. As we proceed through the text, you will see many situations where one loop makes more sense than another.

3.8 Summary
In this chapter you have learned:
- ❏ The basic principles of three different loop structures.
- ❏ Why loop structures make programming more efficient.
- ❏ How each of the loop structures discussed can be implemented in RobotBASIC.
- ❏ How to make our robot draw a line on the floor as it moves.
- ❏ How the `ReadMouse` command can be used to control the robot.

3.9 Exercises
Before moving on to the next chapter, test your knowledge and skill by trying the following exercises. Give each problem your best effort before reviewing the answers given in Appendix A.

1. Describe at least one other everyday situation that fits the logical structure of `for-next`, `while-wend` and `repeat-until` loops.

2. Discuss the changes you made to Figure 3.3 to get a full circle and different sized circles. Explain what worked and why as well as what did not work.

3. The program in Figure 3.6 will stop the robot's movement if you press the LEFT mouse button. Modify the program so that the RIGHT mouse button (instead of the left) can be used to stop the robot.

4. If you run the program in Figure 3.5, you will see that it already works with *either* mouse button. Explain why it works with either button while the program in Figure 3.6 only works with the LEFT button.

Chapter 4

Decisions

We saw in Chapter 3 how loops can make programming more efficient. In this chapter we will expand on some of those basic ideas by creating programs that can make decisions on their own.

Let's start by teaching our robot how to move around a room more intelligently by giving it the ability to become aware of objects in the room and make decisions about how to react to them. We have seen, in previous chapters that an error will be issued when the robot bumps into an object. Our goal is to program the robot so that it can watch for obstacles in its path and avoid them on its own.

> ☑ **Note:** Electro-mechanical devices that do not have sensory capability are not really robots. A remote control robotic toy, for example, is not really a robot because it has no way to examine its environment and cannot make any decisions about its behavior. This does not mean that robots have to have human-level intelligence, but it does mean they have to have *some* capability to deal with *some* situations without human intervention.

In order for our robot to make decisions on its own, it must be able to gather information about its environment. Without this ability, our robot is severely disabled, just as you would be if you were blind and had no sense of touch. Think about this for a moment. If you were disabled this way, how would *you* find your way through a cluttered room?

Giving a robot vision is certainly possible with RobotBASIC (see the vision video on our web page) but it is beyond the skills of a novice programmer.

The RobotBASIC robot is actually much more advanced than we can cover in this introductory text. It has many sensors (including bumper switches, a compass, a GPS, infrared object detection, ultrasonic distance measurement and many others) that can be used to get information about the robot's environment. In this book, we will only utilize a few of these sensors. After you have mastered the material here, you can explore more advanced projects in our book *Robot Programmer's Bonanza* available at most bookstores or on our web page.

4.1 Bumper Switches

Imagine if we had a real robot and wanted it to be able to determine if it has bumped into an object. One simple solution would be to place switches around the perimeter of the robot and build an electronic circuit that allows the controlling computer to determine if those switches have been pressed due to the robot bumping into an object.

The simulated robot in RobotBASIC has four such switches mounted around its perimeter. There is one in front, one in the back and one on each side. The function `rBumper()` checks the status of these switches and returns a number that indicates which switch has contacted an object according to the table below.

Number	Pressed Switch
1	Rear
2	Right side
4	Front
8	Left side

If two switches are pressed simultaneously (this can happen, perhaps, when the robot becomes wedged into a corner) the number returned by rBumper() will be the sum of the numbers for each switch. If we want our program to check if the robot has contacted some object, we can use one of the many forms of IF statements available in RobotBASIC.

4.2 The IF-THEN Structure

The simplest form of the IF is the IF-THEN structure as shown in the example below (the operator <> means 'not equal to').

```
if rBumper() <> 4 then rForward 1
```

When the *expression* following the IF is *true*, then the statement following the THEN is executed. If the expression is *false*, then everything past the THEN is ignored and execution continues on the next line in the program. Think about what the above line really means. If there is nothing in front of the robot (i.e. the front bumper switch is not depressed) then the robot moves forward one pixel. This is a powerful concept that can be applied to many situations.

4.3 The IF-ENDIF Structure

If you have several statements that you want to execute when a given condition is true (instead of just one), then you can use the IF-ENDIF structure shown below. In this example, we are checking to see if the BACK bumper has been pressed. If the expression is true, then all of the statements between the IF and the ENDIF statements will be executed and if the expression is false, then all the statements will be skipped, with execution continuing at the first line following the ENDIF.

```
if rBumper() = 1
        // do the appropriate
        // actions here
endif
```

4.4 The IF-ELSE-ENDIF Structure

In both of the above examples, a statement or group of statements are either executed or skipped. Sometimes, though, we need to execute one group (often called a block) of statements if an expression is true and a different block if the expression is false. This can be done as shown in the example below.

```
if rBumper = 1
        // do these statements
        // if the expression is true
else
        // do these if the
        // if the expression is false
endif
```

Notice that in all these examples, the blocks of statements are indented. This is not required, but it makes the program easier to understand (just like the indenting in loop structures) because it makes it is easier to see all the statements that will be affected by a decision structure.

4.5 The `IF-ELSEIF` Structure

The if-else-endif structure allows us to create actions for two opposite situations, but sometimes programs need to make decisions based on many different conditions. The `if-elseif` structure can handle such situations as shown below.

```
if rBumper=1
        // do these statements
        // if the expression is true
elseif rBumper=2
        // or do these if the new
        // expression is true
elseif rBumper=4
        // or these if this
        // expression is true
else
        // the optional else handles
        // the case of none being true
endif
```

4.6 Designing a Program

Now that we have a basic understanding of several looping and decision structures we can create a program to give our robot a little intelligence. The first step in designing any program is to decide exactly what we want the program to do.

For this example, let's assume we want the robot to move forward until it hits an object. At that point, we want the robot to turn from that object and move away. If we put both of these actions inside an endless loop, the robot should wander aimlessly around its environment. A program to perform these actions is shown in Figure 4.1.

```
// create the robot near the
// center of the screen
rLocate 400,300
while True
    //move forward till bumped
    while rBumper()=0
       rForward 1
    wend
    // now turn away
    rTurn 180
wend
end
```

Figure 4.1: This robot tries to avoid bumping into walls, but fails.

4.7 Explaining the Program

After the robot is located near the center of the screen, an endless `while` loop keeps the robot moving. Remember that a while-loop will keep looping so long as the while-condition evaluates to *true*. So when we say `while True` we are forcing an endless loop since the while-condition will always be true. The words `True` and `False` can be used in decision expressions to force a desired condition. The second (inner) `while` loop causes the robot to inch its way forward.

> **Note:** Having one decision or looping structure inside another is referred to as *nesting*.

The inner `while` loop makes sure that as long as none of the bumpers are pressed (`rBumper()=0`) the robot will continue to move forward.

This action makes sure that the robot never moves more than one pixel before checking the bumper switches again. This is important because the robot will cause an error if it continues to move even one pixel toward an object or wall *after* the bumper has been pressed. You can see this by simply changing the program to make the robot move forward five pixels at a time instead of one.

As long as the robot has not bumped an object, execution of the program will stay inside the inner while-loop. When an object is encountered, the loop will terminate and execution will continue with the statements following the `wend`. At that point, an `rTurn` causes the robot to turn 180°, making the robot turn around and face the direction it came from.

If you enter and run the program, you would expect the robot to move until it hits the top wall, turn around and move until it hits another wall, and so on, continually moving back and forth between the top and bottom walls.

If you run this program, the robot does indeed move forward until it gets to the top wall, but then it just spins around endlessly (type in the program and see for yourself). Unfortunately, this kind of surprising behavior often occurs when doing robotic programs, especially if you are not an experienced programmer. Our next step is to find out why the program does not work the way we expected.

4.8 Debugging the Program

Finding out why programs don't work is a very important aspect of programming called *debugging* or *troubleshooting*. So important in fact, that much of the rest of this chapter will be devoted to finding out why the program is not doing what we intended it to do. Once this is done we need to determine how to fix the problems in the code. By the time we fix all the problems, the robot, and you, should be a lot wiser.

> ☑ **Note:** Programs, even those written by professional programmers, often fail to perform exactly as expected when they are first written. Learning to debug programs is a valuable skill that takes time to master. It is a little like being a detective. You must gather evidence and discover clues about the crime (the programming problem) and then scrutinize those clues to identify potential suspects (logical or syntactical errors in your program). Finally, you must eliminate each suspected problem until you find the guilty culprit.

If you look at the program (Figure 4.1) there is no clearly apparent reason why it should sit and spin once it hits a wall. Study the program to see if you can figure out the problem.

After a little study, you should realize that the robot is probably never executing the `rForward` command. Once you see that, it becomes more obvious why the robot seems to spin. If the robot never moves forward, it will turn 180° away from the wall and then turn another 180° (making it face the wall again). This process will continue over and over making it look like the robot is spinning. Even though it seems clear that this is what is happening, it is important for us to verify it.

One way to verify that our suspicions are correct is to put the delay command shown below into the program right before the inner `while` statement.

```
delay 1000
```

This command will cause the program to pause for 1000 milliseconds (1 second). Make the change and run the program again. You will see that the robot turns away from the wall, then back toward the wall again, over and over, just like we suspected. This gives us confidence that we are on the right track, but the question we now have to answer is *why* is the robot not moving forward after it turns away from the wall? After all, the robot turns away from the wall when a collision occurs, so it is easy to think the robot should be able to move away from the wall. In order to gather clues as to why our logic is faulty, we could place the following statement after the `delay` command.

```
print rBumper()
```

This statement will print the value of the bumper sensors every time the program goes through outer loop. Hopefully, this information can help us see why the robot is not moving forward. If you run the modified program, you will see it print a number every time the robot turns around. The numbers being printed alternate between 1 and 4.

Recall what these numbers mean. A 1 means the back bumper is pressed while a 4 indicates the front bumper. Armed with this new information, we can see why the robot is behaving the way it does.

When the robot reaches the wall, the front bumper is activated and the robot does indeed turn away from the wall. When it turns, though, it rotates around its center, which means that the other bumper switches are pressed as the robot rotates. We never see the numbers for the side sensors because the robot completes a full 180 degree turn before program execution reaches the `print` statement again. You can see all the switches being pressed if you change the `rTurn 180` command to `rTurn 90`.

Now we know the reason why the robot never moves forward. Since one of the sensors is always pressed (once the robot reaches the wall), the inner `while` statement is never TRUE. We must correct this if we want the program to work properly. An easy correction is to make the robot move away from the wall after it turns away but it must do so without any checking any sensors. Once the robot is away from the wall and no bumpers are triggered, the `while` loop should work properly. We can do this by placing the following statement after the `rTurn` command.

rForward 1

With this statement added, the robot will move away from the wall immediately after it turns 180° which means the `while` loop should execute as expected (assuming our logic is correct).

Remove the print and delay statements and try the program again. The robot should move back and forth between the top and bottom walls. It does this, but the totally repetitive action is not very exciting! You might think that making the robot hit the wall at an angle could make our robots behavior more interesting. We can do this by adding the following statement after the `rLocate` statement.

rTurn 20

The robot now moves at an angle, but the robot's behavior is not improved. It still repeats the same path over and over.

4.9 Improving the Program

Each time the robot hits an object, it turns around a full 180°, which is why the repetitive action occurs. We can somewhat fix this problem by simply changing the 180 to something like 160 (so that the robot does not make a complete about-face. If you try this, you will see that the robot does indeed wander around the room, changing directions whenever it hits a wall.

The program is not perfect yet, as the robot still moves away from the wall on a path similar to its approach angle. If we change 160 to 100 it looks a little better, but the robot still turns in the same general direction. Let's see if we can further improve our robot's behavior.

4.10 Adding Randomness

RobotBASIC has a function that generates random numbers as shown in the example below.

```
x = random(30)
```

In this example, the variable **x** will become a number from zero up to, but not including, the parameter provided in the statement. In this example, that means that **x** will assume a value from 0 to 29.

We can utilize this principle in our program to make the robot turn a random amount when it bumps into a wall. For example, assume we want to make the robot turn 180 plus or minus 30°. That means we want the robot to turn some amount between 150° and 210°. This can be done using the following statement.

```
rTurn 150+random(61)
```

If you replace the current rTurn statement with the above line the robot will wander randomly in a reasonable manner. The randomness keeps the robot from reacting the same way all the time, giving it a personality of its own.

Even with this new improved behavior, the robot still has problems. Occasionally it will collide with a wall hitting one of the side bumpers. This can cause a crash because the robot, as it makes a random turn, may actually turn back toward the wall. Ideally, we would prefer that the robot turn directly away from the wall if one of the side bumpers is hit.

We can make this happen if we check to see *which* bumper has been hit and perform different actions accordingly. The program in Figure 4.2 shows one method for implementing this idea. In this program, the robot responds in a random manner (as discussed earlier) whenever the front bumper is activated. If the left bumper (a sensor value of 8) is pressed, the robot turns 90° to the right. Similarly, the robot turns 90° to the left (-90°) if the right bumper (2) is activated. Notice how this logic is implemented with the `if-elseif` decision structure.

```
rLocate 400,300
while True
    // move till bumped
    while rBumper()=0
       rForward 1
    wend
    // now turn away
    if rBumper()=4
       rTurn 150+random (61)
    elseif rBumper()=2
       rTurn -90
    elseif rBumper()=8
       rTurn 90
    endif
    rForward 1
wend
end
```

Figure 4.2: This robot tries to avoid bumping into the walls and works most of the time.

The modified program seems to work great – at least for a while. The robot does turn away from a front collision a random amount. If you watch the robot carefully, you will see that if it hits one of the side bumpers it turns directly left or right, just as we planned. Unfortunately though, if you wait long enough, the robot eventually crashes into a wall or perhaps gets stuck in a corner.

The reason for this is not obvious, so let's try to gather more clues about the robot's undesirable behavior. Add the following line just before the first `if` statement.

```
print rBumper()
```

Now when the robot crashes we can see what number is being reported by the `rBumper()` function. If you modify and run the program, then, depending on how the robot encounters a wall, you will typically see numbers like 12 or 6. As you recall, if more than one bumper is pressed simultaneously then the number reported by `rBumper()` is the sum of the individual bumper numbers.

The number 12, for example, means that both the left and front bumpers are triggered. A 6 implies the front and right bumpers have been hit together. If the robot happens to wedge itself in a corner just right, we would get some other combination of bumper pressings. When any of these numbers is returned by `rBumper()`, our program fails because it does not account for these possibilities. Can you determine why not considering these possibilities causes errors? One way to correct this problem is to add additional `elseif` conditions (and appropriate reactions) to the program.

The idea is to make sure that the robot knows how to respond no matter what situation arises. The program works, but it would be more interesting if we place some objects in the room with the robot so that there is something to bump into besides the walls.

4.11 Summary

In this chapter you have learned:

- ❑ Why real robots need sensory data to make decisions about their behavior.
- ❑ How RobotBASIC's `IF` structures can be used to make decisions.
- ❑ How the techniques used for program debugging can help you determine why a program is not responding as desired.
- ❑ How randomness can give the robot a "personality".

4.12 Exercises

Before moving on to the next chapter, test your knowledge and skill by trying the following exercises. Give each problem your best effort before reviewing the answers given in Appendix A.

1. Type in the program shown in Figure 4.1 and work through the corrections and additions discussed in the chapter.
2. Modify the program in Figure 4.2 by adding additional `elseif` conditions so that the robot never crashes into a wall.
3. After you have a fully working program (see Exercise 2), add several obstacles to the room (see Chapter 2) and see if the robot can avoid them.
4. Modify the randomness aspects of the assignment discussed in Exercise 3 to see if you can create a robot whose behavior you like better.

Chapter 5

Modules

You have probably noticed that the programs we are writing are slowly getting longer and more complicated. As this occurs, it becomes increasingly important that we organize our code so that it is easy to follow the logic of what the program is trying to do.

Any program that you write will be composed of sections that perform one or more functions. In all the programs we have developed so far, the sections were very informal. In this chapter we are going to explore the advantages of dividing up our code into functional modules that will make it easier to design as well as organize our programs.

5.1 Subroutines and Labels

The modules we create in RobotBASIC are called *subroutines* and have the format shown below.

```
NameOfModule:
    // place some code here
    // as many lines as you need
return
```

The name of the module is referred to as a *label*. Labels are case sensitive (like variables) and must be followed by a colon. The code inside the module is usually indented to help identify where it starts and stops. The module must end with a `return` statement.

5.2 The `Gosub` Command

Your program can execute the code contained in a subroutine module by calling it with the following statement.

```
gosub NameOfModule
```

The name of the module is *not* followed by the colon when used with a `gosub` command. When execution in the subroutine reaches the `Return` statement, execution is transferred back to the line following the `gosub` statement that originally called the subroutine.

5.3 Advantages of Modular Programming

Consider for a moment how a large company is organized. The president of the company decides *what* needs to be done in order to achieve the company's goals. The president does not have to know the details of *how* to accomplish many of the tasks that have to be done because there are vice-presidents that handle the details for him.

Let's look at an example. Suppose the president decides the company needs to add a product to their product line. The president goes to the head of manufacturing and asks what changes need to be made to the company's plants and uses that information to command the head of finance to calculate how much new money the company will need as well as alternatives for how the money can be raised. The head of marketing will be responsible for creating an advertising campaign for the new product. The list could go on and on, but you get the idea.

In fact, even the vice presidents don't need to know exactly how to accomplish their respective goals. They have sub-managers and those sub-managers have workers – the people that ultimately do all the work. Everyone above the workers is responsible, not for work, but for decisions, planning, organization and so forth.

This does not mean that the managers are not important. On the contrary, this organizational structure lets each departmental area focus on their tasks and their needs without worrying about other aspects of the project. It is a *divide-and-conquer* strategy that turns a large project into many simple ones.

5.4 Organizing a Program

Programs, especially large programs, need to be organized in the manner described above. Subroutines allow you to combine all the code needed to perform a task and give it a name related to that task. The main portion of your program acts like a manager, calling subroutines when needed to get the job done.

The code in the main portion of a program organized this way will be responsible for deciding *what* needs to be done and *when* (or if) it should be done. Subroutines are called to do the actual work.

As we have seen in previous chapters, the decision portions of a program are composed of control structures like loops and `if` statements. When you utilize a modular style for writing programs, you can get started quickly by concentrating on *what* you want to do without worrying about *how* things will actually be accomplished. This is true, because you can just assume you will have subroutines that can handle the tasks you will need.

Conversely, when you are ready to write the subroutines, you won't have to worry about anything other than solving some specific problem or carrying out some specific task, and if the problem or task is too complex, just write the subroutine as if it is a mid-level manager (that can divide the complex problem into smaller tasks) and let it call other subroutines to handle the actual work.

This organizational structure is a powerful tool that makes programming much easier. Let's look at an example to demonstrate how modular programming can be implemented. Examine the program in Figure 5.1. It is a modularized version of the program we wrote in Chapter 4 (see Figure 4.2).

```
MainProgram:
  gosub Initialize
  while True
    gosub MoveForwardTillBlocked
    gosub TurnAwayFromObject
  wend
end
```

Figure 5.1: This program provides the main logic
for the program shown in Figure 4.2

5.5 Analyzing the Program

Compare the modular organization shown in Figure 5.1 with the program in Figure 4.2. Both programs make the robot perform exactly the same tasks, but it is much easier to see an overview of what is happening in Figure 5.1.

When you write a program with subroutines, the MAIN program *must come first* (followed by the subroutines, *in any order*). In Figure 5.1 the main program is identified with the label **MainProgram**. You may use any label, the exact wording is not important since the label is not being used except as an identifier. But this one is as good as any and helps easily identify the main program at a glance and in making sure that the main program is *always* at the top.

After the initialization, the main program shown in Figure 5.1 enters an endless loop that repeats two actions over and over. These actions are:

- The robot moves forward until it encounters some object.
- The robot turns away from the object.

It is very easy to see how the robot will react to its environment. Of course, once we understand the main program, we must turn our attention to each of the modules that are being called.

Since we can look at each of these modules one at a time, we can focus our attention on how each task can be accomplished without having to worry about the details of other modules. This is a very powerful concept that automatically subdivides large tasks into smaller, manageable ones, making them easier to design and implement.

Of course, for this example, we have already found ways to accomplish each of the required tasks (see Chapter 4). Figure 5.2 shows how the coding details from Figure 4.2 can be organized in a subroutine format.

```
Initialize:
  rLocate 400,300
  LineWidth 4
  Circle 150,200,300,300,Blue,Red
  Rectangle 450,300,600,500,Red,Blue
return

MoveForwardTillBlocked:
  while rBumper()=0
    rForward 1
  wend
return

TurnAwayFromObject:
  if rBumper()=4
    rTurn 150+random(61)
  elseif rBumper()=2
    rTurn -90
  elseif rBumper()=8
    rTurn 90
  endif
  rForward 1
return
```

Figure 5.2: These subroutines do all the work for the main program in Figure 5.1

Most of the code in Figure 5.2 is identical to its counterpart in Figure 4.2. The `Initialize` module, though, was enhanced so that it creates two obstacles in the robot's environment using the `circle` and `rectangle` commands. Notice that these two commands have parameters that we have not used in previous programs.

The first four parameters for `rectangle` (and `circle`) specify the coordinates of the confining space, as described in Chapter 2. The next two parameters are optional. If provided, they specify the edge (line) color and the interior color. If not provided, RobotBASIC uses the default colors set by the `SetColor` command.

The commands in RobotBASIC have been designed so that they are easy to use because many of the parameters in the parameter list are optional. Learning to utilize the optional parameters can make your programming more powerful and more efficient.

5.6 The HELP System

In order to learn what is available in RobotBASIC, as well as what all your options are, you need to become familiar with the HELP system. Activate the HELP screen by clicking on the ❷ button at the top of the screen or by pressing the *F1* key.

You can simply scroll through the HELP information, or you can use the drop-down menu to navigate directly to one of the twenty-four general topic areas available to you. As you become more familiar with programming and RobotBASIC, you also have the option of clicking the 🔍 button (or *Ctrl+F*) to search the entire HELP document for a particular word or phrase.

If you find the rectangle command in the HELP file, you will see the following information.

Rectangle *ne_X1,ne_Y1,ne_X2,ne_Y2{,ne_PenColor{,ne_FillColor}}*
> Draws a rectangle defined by *ne_X1,ne_Y1* and *ne_X2,ne_Y2* filled with *ne_FillColor* and bordered with *ne_PenColor*. If the colors are not given then the default background color will be used for filling and the pen color for the border. If you want to specify the fill color you must also give the pen color but any color value less than 0 will be ignored. *ne_X1,ne_Y1* are coordinates on the screen of the top left corner, and *ne_X2,ne_Y2* are of the bottom right corner of the rectangle.

Notice that each of the variables in the parameter list is preceded by **ne_**. This notation is explained elsewhere in the HELP file and indicates that the variable in question can be any expression (such as x, x+3, etc.) that results in a numeric value. As we proceed through later chapters, you will discover other options that parameters can have.

The important point here is that the RobotBASIC help system contains a wealth of information that can help you discover far more power than we can fully discuss in any book. All this information can be overwhelming at first, especially if you are new to programming. The more you use it though the more comfortable you will become and soon you will be able to find the information you need with a few clicks of the mouse.

5.7 Summary
In this chapter you have learned:
- ❑ Why modular programming techniques create a better organized program that is easier to read and understand.
- ❑ How subroutines can be used to implement a modular design.
- ❑ How the gosub statement can force the execution of subroutines.
- ❑ That the RobotBASIC HELP file contains an enormous amount of valuable information.

5.8 Exercises

Before moving on to the next chapter, test your knowledge and skill by trying the following exercises. Give each problem your best effort before reviewing the answers given in Appendix A.

1. Type in the program shown in Figures 5.1 and 5.2 and verify that it works as described.

2. Modify the program in Exercise 1 so that it has two additional obstacles for the robot to avoid. Also, make appropriate changes (as described in Chapter 4) so the robot does not crash into walls when two of the bumpers are contacted simultaneously.

3. Locate information on the REPEAT-UNTIL loop and the SetColor command in the HELP file and summarize something new that you have learned about the statements.

Chapter 6

Using the Mouse

C hapter 5 stressed the need for proper organization when writing a program, but it was difficult to see the real value of the principles discussed with the small programs used in that chapter. In this chapter we will begin writing larger, more complex programs which will make the need for and the power of modular programming more evident.

Even though the overall programs will be more complex, the programming will not be daunting since the individual modules (subroutines) will be easy to understand and create just as we have done so far.

6.1 Moving Objects with the Mouse

The first program for this chapter will draw two shapes (a circle and a square) on the screen. The user will be allowed to select one of the objects (by clicking the mouse on it) and then move the object around the screen (by dragging the mouse while the button is pressed).

As stated earlier, this program is complex enough that the value of modular techniques can be appreciated. Look at the main program in Figure 6.1.

6.2 The Main Program

The program begins by performing some initialization and then enters an endless loop. Inside the loop a subroutine is called that decides if either of the shapes has been selected (by moving the mouse over the shape and pressing a mouse button).

```
MainProgram:
  gosub Initialization
  while True
    gosub CheckMouse
    if Selected=1
        gosub MoveCircle
    elseif Selected=2
        gosub MoveSquare
    endif
  wend
end
```

Figure 6.1: This main program acts as a supervising manager that calls on workers to perform tasks.

After the **CheckMouse** subroutine determines which shape was chosen, it has to pass that information back to the main program. During the design of this program, it was decided that the information would be passed by setting the value of the variable **Selected** to 1 if the circle was selected and 2 if the square was chosen.

6.3 The Power of Modularity

Notice that we can program the primary functionality of our entire program in this MAIN module without programming any of the subordinate modules. Of course, we have to decide *what* each module will do, but we don't have to concern ourselves (at this point) with the details of *how* the modules will do their jobs.

Once the main program knows which object was selected (based on the value of the variable **Selected**), an `if` control structure can decide which object to move (which is handled by calling one of two appropriately named subroutines).

Examine the main program again carefully. The power of what we have just described is extraordinary. We can read this short section of code and determine the overall operation of our entire program. Also, the organization of this module has divided a relatively complex problem into the four simpler problems described below.

6.4 Module Definitions

Initialization: This module will create the robot and setup the initial positions of the circle and square before drawing both objects on the screen.

CheckMouse: This module will check to see if a mouse button is pressed. If not, the module will just return to the main module with the variable **Selected** set to zero. If the button is pressed, then the module will decide if the mouse pointer is over one of the objects and sets the value of **Selected** to 1 or 2 appropriately. If an object has been selected, the variables **x** and **y** will be set to the current mouse position.

MoveCircle: This module will erase the currently drawn circle from the screen and then redraw the circle at the position specified by **x,y** (the current mouse position).

MoveSquare: This module will erase the currently drawn square from the screen and then redraw the square at the position specified by **x,y** (the current mouse position).

The above descriptions help simplify the creation of each of these modules because the details of what each subroutine must do are becoming more specific. Figure 6.2

shows an implementation for these modules. Let's look at the details of each module, starting with **Initialization**.

The **Initialization** module starts by establishing the size of the objects in this program by setting the variable **s** to 15. We will see later how this variable controls the size of the objects. For now though, just accept that you can change the size of both objects by simply changing the value of this variable.

```
Initialization:
  // set up starting postions and size
  s=15 // size of objects
  cx=200
  cy=200
  sx=400
  sy=400
  LineWidth 3
  gosub DrawCircle
  gosub DrawSquare
return

CheckMouse:
  Selected=0
  ReadMouse x,y,b
  if b=0 then return
  if within(x,cx-s,cx+s) and within(y,cy-s,cy+s)
    Selected=1
  elseif within(x,sx-s,sx+s) and within(y,sy-s,sy+s)
    Selected=2
  endif
return

MoveCircle:
  gosub EraseCircle
  cx=x
  cy=y
  gosub DrawCircle
return

MoveSquare:
  gosub EraseSquare
  sx=x
  sy=y
  gosub DrawSquare
return
```

Figure 6.2: These modules perform tasks as requested by the main program in Figure 6.1.

In the design of this program, the current x,y location of the circle will be defined by **cx,cy**. The square's location will be **sx,sy**. The Initialization module sets initial values for all four of these variables and then draws the objects by calling additional subroutines that know how to perform this action. This hierarchal nesting is an important concept. The main program was simplified by utilizing subordinate modules to perform the needed actions. Now we see, that even the subordinate modules can be simplified by letting them delegate things they need to do, to additional subroutines. This technique also simplifies the coding for **MoveCircle** and **MoveSquare**.

Both of these modules start by calling a module that will erase the object being moved (at its current location). The object is then redrawn at the current mouse position (by setting the object's coordinates to the current mouse coordinates and then calling a routine that draws the object). Of course, we still have to create modules such as **EraseCircle** and **DrawSquare** that can erase and draw their respective shape at the shape's specified position (**cx,cy** and **sx,sy**).

6.5 Finding if the Mouse is Over an Object

This leaves only one module in Figure 6.2 to examine. One of the primary actions of the **CheckMouse** module is to decide if the mouse cursor is over one of the objects. Before we can write the code to handle such a task, we must determine some method or principle for actually accomplishing this task.

Let's start with what we know. Based on the information previously provided, we know the mouse's position is **x,y** and the circle is located at **cx,cy** and the square is at **sx,sy**. We also know that size of our objects is specified by the variable **s**. Based on this information, we can formulate a plan or *algorithm* to determine if the mouse is over a particular object.

We certainly could assume the mouse is over the circle, if the coordinates of the mouse and the circle were the same. This could be checked with a statement such as the one below.

```
if x=cx and y=cy
```

We could perform the check this way, but the statement above would only be true if mouse was in the *exact* same position as the circle (the mouse cursor would have to be in the very center of the circle). Obviously, it would be better if we could have a little tolerance when we try to select an object.

The first question that should come to mind is "how much tolerance". Since we know the size of our objects is stored in the variable **s**, let's use that as a reasonable guess at an appropriate tolerance. We need a way then, to make sure that each of the respective coordinates are within **s** of each other. We could check the x-coordinates with the following line.

```
if (x>cx-s) and (x<cx+s)
```

Let's examine the logic of the above line. Remember, **cx** specifies the horizontal position of the circle and **x** specifies the horizontal position of the mouse. The formulas **cx-s** and **cx+s** specify positions on the screen that are above and below the primary location of the circle and the `if` statement above is simply seeing if **x** is greater than the smaller of these numbers *and* less than the larger.

Of course, to make sure the mouse is over the circle, we must verify both the x and y coordinates. This could be done with a statement like this:

```
if ((x>cx-s) and (x<cx+s)) and ((y>ys-s) and (y<cs+s))
```

Notice how the expressions being ANDed together are each enclosed in parenthesis. This is not always required, but it never hurts to help the computer see where you want an expression to begin and end. The computer is more likely to misinterpret complex expressions if they don't have parenthesis. The HELP file has lots of information concerning the evaluation of expressions. Consult it as you progress to more complex programming situations.

We can certainly utilize the logic shown above, but this type of decision occurs so often in programs that RobotBASIC offers a special function to make things easier. This function requires three parameters as shown in the example below.

```
within(a,b,c)
```

The above function will be true if the value of **a** is between the values of **b** and **c**. This means we could check to see if the mouse was over the circle with this statement.

```
if within(x,cx-s,cx+s) and within(y,cy-s,cy+s)
```

Now that we understand how we can determine when the mouse is over an object, it will be easy to see how the **CheckMouse** subroutine works. Refer to Figure 6.2 for the following discussion.

The first thing the subroutine does is set **Selected** to zero, thus making the assumption that the mouse is not over either of the objects. Next, the ReadMouse() function sets the variables **x** and **y** to the current mouse position and **b** to the status of the mouse buttons. If none of the mouse buttons are pressed, then the subroutine returns (with **Selected** indicating that no object has been selected).

If a button is pressed, the **CheckMouse** module uses an if structure to decide what value to assign to **Selected** before returning to the main program.

Hopefully the logic of each of these routines is easy to follow. If you have any trouble understanding *any* of this material, go back over everything in this chapter until it is fully clear to you. Understanding the principles discussed in this chapter is essential if you are going to be a good programmer.

6.6 Drawing and Erasing Objects

If you are following the logic of this program, you know we are not quite finished yet. There are still four subroutines that we have not coded. They are shown in Figure 6.3 and should not be difficult to understand.

Each object is drawn centered around its x,y coordinates. The corners of the rectangle are calculated by adding and subtracting **s**, the size of the objects (making the objects 2***s** on each side). When the objects are drawn, the circle is drawn with a blue interior and a red perimeter while the square is drawn in the opposite way. In order to erase an object, it is simply drawn in WHITE, which is the background color of the screen.

```
DrawCircle:
  // centered at cx,cy
  circle cx-s,cy-s,cx+s,cy+s,RED,BLUE
return

DrawSquare:
  // centered at sx,sy
  rectangle sx-s,sy-s,sx+s,sy+s,BLUE,RED
return

EraseCircle:
  // centered at cx,cy
  circle cx-s,cy-s,cx+s,cy+s,WHITE,WHITE
return

EraseSquare:
  // centered at sx,sy
  rectangle sx-s,sy-s,sx+s,sy+s,WHITE,WHITE
return
```

Figure 6.3: These subroutines handle the task of drawing and erasing objects for several subroutines in the sample program.

Type in all the parts of the program and run it. If you make any mistakes as you type, you might get some errors. Utilize the debugging principles we discussed in previous chapters to find the problems and correct them. When you run the program, you should be able to move the mouse cursor over either of the objects and then select it by holding down one of the mouse buttons. If you keep the mouse button pressed as you move the mouse, you will be able to drag the selected object around the screen.

6.7 Principles of Animation

The way these shapes move around the screen (erasing and redrawing) is the basis for the animation you see in simulations and video games. In fact, the simulated robot in RobotBASIC moves in this manner. If you are interested in graphical animation and video games, please consider our book *RobotBASIC Projects for Beginners*, available on our web page. Like this book, it teaches the fundamentals of programming, but the example applications concentrate on graphics and video games rather than robotics.

6.8 Summary

In this chapter you have learned:

- ❑ How the mouse can be used to move objects around the screen.
- ❑ How nested subroutines can make the logic of a program easier to understand.
- ❑ How the within() function can simplify some complex decision operations.
- ❑ The basic principles of graphical animation.

6.9 Exercises

Before moving on to the next chapter, test your knowledge and skill by trying the following exercises. Give each problem your best effort before reviewing the answers given in Appendix A.

1. Type in the program described in this chapter and verify that it functions correctly.

2. Modify the program in this chapter so that ONLY the LEFT mouse button can be used to select an object.

3. Change the size of the objects used in the program described in this chapter.

4. Modify the program in the chapter so that ONLY the square is larger.

5. The program in this chapter will erase the other shape if you make the dragged shape draw over it. Can you think of a way to stop this from happening?

> **Hint:** Redraw the other shape as well.

6. Create a modular program that allows you to control the robot with the mouse. Have the robot wander around the room (taking random turns when it encounters a wall), but have the robot make gentle turns left and right as long as the left or right mouse button is pressed.

> **Hint:** You can create a gentle turn by doing this:
> ```
> rForward 1
> rTurn 1
> ```

Chapter 7

Following a Line

By this point in the book, you should be developing an understanding for what programming is all about. Hopefully it is not nearly as difficult as you might have expected. After all, you are simply learning a language that the computer can understand so that you can give it instructions as to what you want it to do.

As you have seen, you do have to be very specific when you give the computer instructions because it only does what you tell it to do. If you forget some small detail or if you tell it wrongly, the robot will blindly obey your commands.

Obviously, though, you can't tell the computer what to do if you don't know how to do it yourself. In this chapter we will examine a complex enough problem that you won't know how to do it yourself. This will provide the opportunity to learn how to develop a plan or *algorithm* through trial and error so that you can create a program that allows the robot to utilize the intelligence you develop.

7.1 Line Following

The problem we are going to examine is how to teach our robot to follow a line on the floor. The first order of business is to actually draw the line. Figure 7.1 shows an

initialization subroutine that draws the line and locates the
robot on top of it.

```
Initialization:
  LineWidth 10
  SetColor GREEN
  Line 100,500,100,400
  LineTo 120,300
  LineTo 140,250
  LineTo 160,175
  LineTo 180,150
  LineTo 200,130
  LineTo 225,120
  LineTo 250,100
  LineTo 300,90
  LineTo 350,110
  LineTo 450,90
  LineTo 600,200
  LineTo 500,330
  LineTo 600,450
  LineTo 550,500
  LineTo 350,550
  LineTo 100,500
  rLocate 100,500
  rInvisible GREEN
return
```

Figure 7.1: This subroutine draws a line on the
screen and initializes the robot on the line.

The line drawn by Figure 7.1 is green and ten pixels wide.
After the robot is located directly on the line, the color
GREEN is designated as an invisible color so that the robot
will not see it as a wall or obstacle. Figure 7.2 shows the
line with the robot on it. Since the line is a loop, a properly
functioning robot should be able to follow the line
indefinitely.

You will notice that the line has both left and right turns
as well as gentle curves and sharp corners. This gives us a
reasonably diverse set of conditions for testing our ideas.

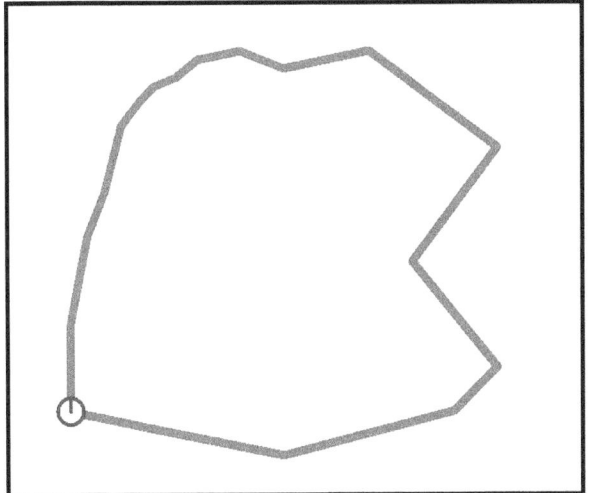

Figure 7.2: This is the line our robot will follow.

Figure 7.3 shows the basic framework or *template* for our main program. All we have to do now is write the **FollowLine** module.

```
MainProgram:
  gosub Initialization
  gosub FollowLine
end
```

Figure 7.3: This is the main program for our line follower.

In order to write the **FollowLine** subroutine, we must know how to follow the line ourselves, otherwise how can we possibly tell the robot how to do it. It is very important for you to put yourself in the robot's place and imagine how the world looks from that point of view.

7.2 Line Sensors

The simulated robot has three line-sensors located immediately in front of the robot. The middle sensor is directly forward, while the other two are slightly left and right of center (and just a little behind the middle sensor). Each of these sensors indicates a 1 if it sees a line and 0 if it doesn't. The outputs of all three sensors are organized into a single number as shown in Figure 7.4.

Which Sensors Are ON	Sensors L M R	Decimal Equivalent
None	0 0 0	0
Right only	0 0 1	1
Middle only	0 1 0	2
Middle & Right	0 1 1	3
Left only	1 0 0	4
Left & Right	1 0 1	5
Left & Middle	1 1 0	6
All	1 1 1	7

Figure 7.4: Table of all possible combinations of sensors' outputs.

7.3 Binary Numbers

The *decimal numbering system* developed by humans has ten elements called digits (0-9), because we originally learned to count using our ten fingers. There are other numbering systems that use a different number of elements. The circuits used to build computers generally only deal with two states (**on** or **off**, **true** or **false**). For that reason, the internal mathematics of computers and computer languages is based on a system with two elements, called the *binary numbering system*. The two elements used in the binary system are 1 and 0 and are referred to as *bits*.

7.4 The `rSense()` Function

RobotBASIC uses the function `rSense()` to read the value of the robot's three line sensors. Each of the line sensor's condition (1 or 0) make up one of the bits in the number returned by `rSense()`, with the left sensor being the most significant bit (MSB) which is the leftmost one. The least significant bit (LSB) is the rightmost one.

The middle column of Figure 7.4 shows all the possible binary number combinations that can occur with the three bits returned by the three sensors (their decimal equivalents are shown in the right column). These numbers indicate how our robot is situated over the line. Using these numbers we can write a program that enables our robot to decide which way to turn so as to stay on the line while it is moving forward and not get too far right or left of it. If you are going to tell the robot how to make such decisions, you must learn how to follow the line yourself, using the same limited information available to the robot - the value returned by rSense() in this case. Let's try an experiment to help you see the line from the robot's point of view.

7.5 Developing an Algorithm

Take a 3 by 5 card or a small piece of paper and punch three holes in a row near the center of the paper. Separate the holes by a space roughly equivalent to the size of the holes. Now take a large piece of paper or poster board and draw a curved line on it with a width slightly wider than the width of all three holes together, as shown in Figure 7.5.

If you look closely at the card in Figure 7.5, you will see that you can see the line through two of the holes, but not through the right-hand hole. This situation is characterized by the number 6 (110). For the next step, choose another person to be your partner and work as a team.

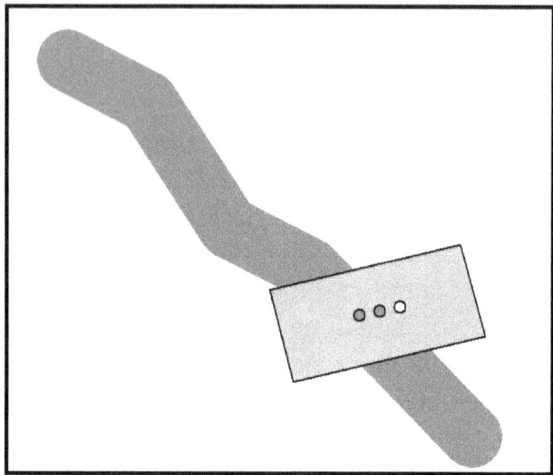

Figure 7.5: Use a 3 by 5 card with holes to help
you learn how to follow a line.

One person on the team should move the card and report
what number is indicated by the holes (use the table in
Figure 7.4). The second person on the team should be
positioned so as to not be able to see the card or the line.
She or he listens to the numbers being reported, and then
tells the person moving the card to do one of the following
(using the table in Figure 7.4).

- move the card forward slightly
- turn the card slightly clockwise
- turn the card slightly counterclockwise

Notice that these actions are things the robot can do.
Notice also that the information being provided from the
card is something the robot can obtain. This means that we
can program the robot to follow the line if you can learn to
follow the line using only the numbers given by your
partner. Before you continue reading, try the above
experiment and see if you can figure out an algorithm for
following the line.

7.6 A Simple Approach

With a little effort, you can come up with lots of ideas. One simple approach, you may have thought of is to have the robot turn back towards the line every time it starts deviating from it.

We can tell that the robot is getting off the line on the left side if rSense() is returning the number 3 (refer to Figure 7.4). If it is, we will want the robot to turn right, or clockwise. If a 6 is being return (like in Figure 7.5) we would want the robot to turn left to bring it back onto the line. If all of the sensors are on the line (7), then the robot should just move forward. The **FollowLine** subroutine in Figure 7.6 shows how these ideas can be implemented in code.

There is something about this code that deserves a closer look. Instead of testing the function rSense() in each of the if conditions, the sensor data is stored into the variable **a** before the testing begins, then the value of **a** can be tested instead of calling the function every time. This is a much more efficient way for programming this particular situation.

```
FollowLine:
  while True
    a=rSense()
    if a=3
      rTurn 1
    elseif a=6
      rTurn -1
    elseif a=7
      rForward 1
    endif
  wend
return
```

Figure 7.6: This subroutine is a good attempt at developing a line following algorithm.

If you enter Figures 7.1, 7.3, and 7.6 and run the program, you will see that the robot does indeed follow the line, at least for a while. When it gets to a sharp turn it fails to turn fast enough and appears to just stop. We need to find out exactly why the robot is not moving.

7.7 Another Debugging Tool

Close the output window and then choose the RUN menu option at the top of editor screen. When the menu drops down, select the VIEW VARIABLE TABLE option, which will display all of the variables being used by the program with the values they had when you stopped the program. You will see that the current value of **a** is 1. Refer to the table in Figure 7.4 to see what that means. A value of 1 means that only the right-most sensor is seeing the line. The other two sensors are not being triggered. If you look at the robot after it has stopped, it is easy to see how this situation can happen (you can bring the Terminal screen back up to see the robot again by pressing the ◀ button).

When a sharp turn is encountered, the robot needs to turn faster. If it doesn't, then the robot sees less and less of the line as it tries (but fails) to get back on the line. We need our program to check for this condition (as well as the similar condition on the opposite side of the line) and handle it in some manner. The question becomes, how should the robot respond to this condition.

One simple option would be for the robot to turn 2° instead of 1° as we have for the other conditions. This makes some sense. If the robot is off the line just a little turn back one degree. If the robot is off a lot, then turn back two degrees.

Of course, just because it makes sense does not mean that it will work. The only way to know is to write some code and test our idea. Figure 7.7 shows a new **FollowLine** subroutine with these modifications implemented. Note, the changes are shown in bold.

To try this code, replace the old **FollowLine** subroutine with the one in Figure 7.7 and run the program again.

With these modifications, the robot does make it through the first two sharp corners, but then stops again as before. When it does, look at the variable table to determine what the sensors are reading. You should see a 5 for the value of **a**. We know from the table in Figure 7.4 that a value of 5 means the left and right sensors are triggered, but not the middle one. This is an unusual and certainly unexpected situation. The only reason it could happen is that the middle sensor is actually slightly forward of the other two (as mentioned earlier).

```
FollowLine:
  while True
    a=rSense()
    if a=3
       rTurn 1
    elseif a=6
       rTurn -1
    elseif a=1
       rTurn 2
    elseif a=4
       rTurn -2
    elseif a=7
       rForward 1
    endif
  wend
return
```

Figure 7.7: This subroutine is a *little* better than the algorithm in Figure 7.6.

We can easily detect this condition, but how do we handle it. Since both the left *and* right sensors are triggered, how do we decide which way to turn? If we think about it for a bit, about the only logical solution is to have the robot simply turn the same way it did the *last* time it turned. Let's see why that makes sense.

If the robot was turning left, for example, when a sensor value of 5 occurred, does it not make sense that the robot should just keep doing what it was doing, until it gets back on the line? This is at least an idea to try, but how do we know which way the robot has been turning. After all, that was something that happened in the past.

If you need to remember something, how do you handle it? You might, for example, write things down that you need to remember. Let's see how we can let the robot do this too. Refer to Figure 7.8.

7.8 Making the Robot Remember

In this version of the subroutine, we introduce a new variable **LT** which stands for *last turn*. In this variable we are going to store the direction of the turn that the robot took as it turns. This way next time when we need to recall what the direction of the last turn was, we can see what it was by looking at the value stored in the LT variable. In every `if` block that makes the robot turn right we will set **LT** equal to 1 (i.e. right turn). In every block where the robot turns left we will set **LT** equal to -1 (i.e. left turn). This means that we can just tell the robot to perform an `rTurn LT` when a sensor condition of 5 is detected (see the new subroutine in Figure 7.8).

If you again replace the old subroutine with the new one from Figure 7.8 and run the program, it will work perfectly the first time round the loop, but the next time round the loop it stops again. Viewing the variables table again tells us the condition causing the problem. The fault occurs when none of the sensors are on the line (**a=0**). This condition (a sensor value of 0) is almost the last possibility to test. The only remaining condition is a value of 2.

```
FollowLine:
  while True
    a=rSense()
    if a=3
      rTurn 1
      LT=1
    elseif a=6
      rTurn -1
      LT=-1
    elseif a=1
      rTurn 2
      LT=1
    elseif a=4
      rTurn -2
      LT=-1
    elseif a=5
      rTurn LT
    elseif a=7
      rForward 1
    endif
  wend
return
```

Figure 7.8: This subroutine is almost perfect, but it still fails in some situations.

Now we must decide what the robot should do when NONE of the sensors see the line. After a little thought, it seems reasonable to have the robot continue turning just as we did for condition 5. Perhaps, we should go ahead and test for a sensor value of 2 also. Perhaps it makes sense to have it turn in the last direction taken as well. This is an easy change, so let's try it and see how our robot responds.

Since we already have a test for **a=5**, we can just change that line as follows:

```
elseif a=5 or a=0 or a=2
```

This will cause all three of these conditions to make the robot turn just as it did in the recent past. Make this change and you will see the robot run around the loop over and over with no problems.

7.9 The Value of Simulation

The logical process demonstrated in this example is what programming is all about. When a program fails to perform, you must gather information about the fault and adjust your code to properly handle every possible situation that might occur.

Often, when you are working with a real robot (the book *Robot Programmer's Bonanza* shows how real robots can be controlled with RobotBASIC) it can be very difficult to determine why it does not respond as you expect. There are many reasons for this, but let's look at a couple.

In real-world situations, it is difficult to get the robot to exactly repeat what it is doing. When you can't duplicate an error situation it can be difficult if not impossible to set up tests to find out why problems are occurring. Also, most languages used to control hobby robots are microcontroller-based, and have limited debugging capabilities. RobotBASIC has debugging capabilities beyond the scope of this text, so refer to the HELP system as you become more experienced.

7.10 Finding the Line

The robot now follows the line perfectly, but you might be wondering how the robot could find the line initially, assuming it was not placed on the line from the start.

If you just locate the robot at 300,500 (or somewhere else off the line) we can see how our current algorithm responds. If you try this, you will get a VARIABLE NOT INITIALIZED error. When you close the terminal window to get back to the editor you see that the variable in question is **LT**.

This makes sense, because the robot never makes any turns before executing this line, and if no turns are made, **LT** will not have been assigned a value, thus causing the error. Let's try to make the robot capable of finding the line on its own. Start by adding the following line at the end of the **Initialization** subroutine. We will use an initial value of zero so that the robot does not have a preset direction to turn.

$$LT=0$$

If you run the program now, there is no error, but the robot just sits quietly. This problem is easy to debug because our program is properly organized.

We know that the robot's sensors are returning zero if the robot is not on the line (which it is not). If we examine our program to see what the robot is supposed to do when the sensors return zero, we see it simply turns **LT** degrees. In order to make sure the robot always moves forward in this situation add an `rForward 1` after the `rTurn`.

Running the program now causes the robot to move forward, find the line, and (depending on what sensors hit the line first) turn onto the line and follow it as before. Or, perhaps we should say *almost* as before.

Because of the additional `rForward` command we added, the robot does not turn as quickly as it used to when this condition occurs. This means that occasionally the robot looses the line when it tries to make a sharp turn. The good news is that even when the line is lost, the robot knows which direction it was turning, and (in a looping manner) makes its way back to the line.

7.11 Compromises

This last change is a good example of how programmers sometimes have to make compromises. In this case, we can either have the robot stay properly on the line without the ability to find the line or we can have a robot that can find a line on its own, but has trouble staying on the line during sharp turns.

You have to examine your particular application in order to decide what behaviors are acceptable. Sometimes simple compromises are okay, and sometimes you just have to knuckle down and find new and better solutions to your problems.

7.12 Summary

In this chapter you have learned:

❑ How rSense() can return information about a line drawn on the floor of the robot's environment.

❑ How binary numbers relate to decimal numbers and why they are used by computers.

❑ How algorithms are developed by observing the robot's reaction to its environment.

❑ How the robot can remember its past actions and use that information to shape its future actions.

❑ How the variables table can be viewed to get additional debugging information.

❑ Why a simulation is a valuable tool for developing robotic algorithms.

7.13 Exercises

Before moving on to the next chapter, test your knowledge and skill by trying the following exercises. Give each problem your best effort before reviewing the answers given in Appendix A.

1. Type in the programs described in this chapter and make sure they operate as described

2. One of the options in the chapter produced a robot that could find a line once it lost it. Modify the line-drawing portion of this program to produce two breaks in the line and test the program to find out if it can handle breaks, and if so, how large a break can be tolerated.

3. The algorithms developed in this chapter assume the line to be followed is wider than the combined width of all the line sensors. How do you think these programs would respond to thinner lines? Create your own algorithm, or modify this one, to make a robot that can follow a thinner line, perhaps 4 pixels wide.

Chapter 8

Finding an Object

Previous chapters have taught our robot to feel its way around a room and follow a line on the floor. In this chapter we want to give the robot some limited vision so it can search its environment for objects of interest.

It is important to realize that full human-style vision is complex and certainly beyond this introductory text. You might be surprised though, at how much functionality some simple commands can provide.

8.1 Vision Commands

RobotBASIC has the ability to capture images from TWAIN-compliant web cams, so as your programming skills grow, you should explore the HELP file to learn more about the advanced commands and functions that can help you achieve complex projects. For now though, lets look at two functions that can give our robot some limited sight.

8.2 The rLook() Function

The rLook() function assumes the robot has some form of camera that can detect colors. It returns the numeric code for the *first* color seen directly in front of the robot. This means that objects hidden behind other objects cannot be seen (just like human vision). Invisible colors, such as a line drawn on the floor are ignored. In general, this function allows you to look for objects that have a unique color.

8.3 The `rBeacon()` Function

The `rBeacon()` function was designed to simulate an infrared detector designed to detect modulated infrared beacons strategically placed in a room. The beacon can be used for navigation in much the same way that a boat uses a lighthouse.

This function requires one parameter, which is the color representing the beacon. Invisible colors are *not* ignored, which allows you to imagine the beacon is mounted near the ceiling so it does not interfere with the robot's movements. The high mounting also means the beacon can be seen even if there are objects on the floor between the robot and the beacon.

The function `rBeacon()` can be used in two ways. If all you want to know is whether the beacon can be seen, the returned value can be thought of as True or False. If you want to simulate a more advanced sensor, the value returned will be zero (False) if no beacon is seen and the distance to the beacon (in pixels) if it is seen.

8.4 Using Simulated Sensors

It is important to realize that you can use either of the above commands in anyway you want. They were designed to emulate specific hardware that can be purchased or built for a real robot, but feel free to dream up new ways of using them. In general, any reasonable sensor that you can imagine can be built or purchased. One of the big advantages of using a simulator is that you can find out what features you want in your sensors *before* you begin physical construction.

8.5 Finding an Object

Let's look at a simple example to show how we can use
`rLook()` to detect a RED object in an empty room.
Imagine you are the robot. If you could detect colors
directly in front of you, how would you look for a RED
object? The answer should be easy. You would simply
turn around, until you see the object. Figure 8.1 shows how
we can create a subroutine that can make the robot do
exactly that.

```
LookForRed:
   xyString 10,580,"Looking "
   for a=1 to 360
      rTurn 1
      if rLook()=Red then break
   next
   if rLook()=Red then gosub GoToIt
return
```

Figure 8.1: This subroutine can find a RED object.

There are some new ideas in Figure 8.1. Ignore the
`xyString` command for now; it will be discussed later.
Let's look at the `for` loop, which repeats 360 times (the
number of degrees in a full circle). Since there is an `rTurn`
`1` command inside the loop, the robot will turn one
complete revolution, allowing it to see the entire room.

The `if` statement inside the loop does the important
work. It calls the `rLook()` function and checks if it can
see the RED object. If a RED object is seen, the statement
is True, so the `break` command is executed.

We have not used the `break` command before. When
executed inside a loop, it forces the loop to end early, with
execution continuing, in this case, at the first line following
the next. This means that the robot will attempt to turn a
full circle looking for the object, but, if it sees the object
during the turn, it will stop with the robot facing the object
(and terminate the `for` loop).

This means that the loop can finish in one of two ways. If it breaks early, then a RED object has been found. If the loop comes to a natural end though, the robot has completed a full turn without seeing the object. How do we know which way the loop ended? An easy solution is to check rLook() again. This allows us to call another subroutine to actually go to the object if one is within view.

8.6 Moving to the Object After it is Found

The next step is to create the **GoToIt** subroutine, which could be as simple as just moving the robot forward until it bumps into an object, but what if there are other objects in the room. Imagine the robot only being able to get a glimpse of a red circle as shown in Figure 8.2. Even though the circle can be seen, the rectangle will block the path and keep the robot from getting to the object (assuming the robot simply moves forward).

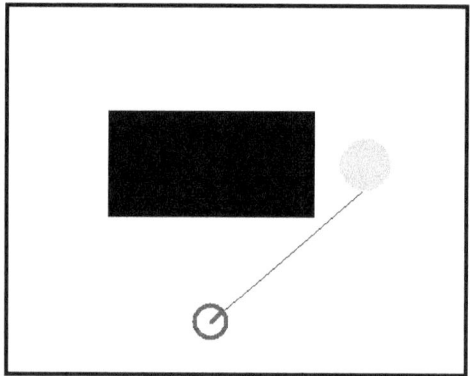

Figure 8.2: Just because the robot can see an object, does not mean it can get to it.

This means that we can't just move the robot forward until it bumps an object, because we can't be sure the object bumped is the RED one the robot is trying to find. Figure 8.3 shows one possible solution to this problem.

```
GoToIt:
  xyString 10,580,"Go to it"
  while rBumper()=0
    rForward 1
  wend
  if rBeacon(RED)>0 and rBeacon(RED)<15
    Found=true
  endif
return
```

Figure 8.3: This subroutine tries to move to a RED object, and lets you know if it succeeded.

The code in Figure 8.3 is only called by the code in Figure 8.1 if the RED object is directly in front of the robot. It is reasonable therefore, for the robot to simply move forward until it bumps into an object. This is accomplished with the while loop.

8.7 Knowing the Object Has Been Found

Once an object has been encountered, the robot must decide if the RED object has been reached. This is not a trivial problem. We can't just assume we are at the object if we can see it. Even when the robot is stopped by the rectangle in Figure 8.2, it can still see the RED circle.

One solution is to use rBeacon() to measure the distance to the RED object (refer to Section 8.3) after the bump has occurred. If the distance is small, we can assume we have found our object. The distance must be greater than 0, because rBeacon() returns 0 if the specified color is not seen at all. The distance must also be relatively small, so we know we have arrived. How small, depends on the size and shape of the RED object.

If we assume the RED object is a circle of radius 15, then it is possible that the robot is seeing just the edge of the object (see Figure 8.2). If the line-of-sight is at the very edge, then the robot could be nearly 15 pixels away when the bump occurs. The `if` statement in Figure 8.3 shows how to determine if the robot has indeed collided with the RED circle.

If the object has been found, then the variable **Found** is set to **True**. We will soon see how this variable will be used. For now, let's test our program by combining Figures 8.1 and 8.3 with the code in Figure 8.4 (remember **MainProgram** must always be at the top).

```
MainProgram:
  gosub Initialize
  Found=False
  repeat
    gosub LookForRed
  until Found
  xyString 10,580,"Found It"
end

Initialize:
  // create an object to find
  // choose from two places
  s=15
  if random(100)<50
    circle 700-s,100-s,700+s,100+s,RED,RED
  else
    circle 300-s,500-s,300+s,500+s,RED,RED
  endif
  // create robot
  rLocate 300,300
return

// add Figures 8.1 and 8.3 here
```

Figure 8.4: This subroutine can find a RED object.

First, let's look at the main program in Figure 8.4. After initialization, the variable **Found** is set to **False**. This will force the `repeat-until` loop to continue until the object is found (recall, that **Found** is set to **True** when the object is found).

8.8 Printing Anywhere You Want

After the loop, an `xyString` command is executed. Now is a good time to explain this new statement. It acts like a print statement, but you can specify exactly where you want the information to be printed. The first two parameters are the x,y position (in pixels) where the printing will start.

The `xyString` statement was used in both the **LookForRed** and **GoToIt** subroutines. In this program, we are simply printing what the robot is doing (example: *Looking* or *Going to it*) so that the user will know for sure what the robot is trying to do. As we improve this program, this will make more sense. Notice that we are printing each new phrase in the exact same position on the screen. If we pad the end of each phrase with an appropriate number of spaces, we can ensure that each new phrase will erase the old one (since it is printed on top of it).

Turn your attention to the **Initialize** routine in Figure 8.4. It will create our RED object in one of two places. It decides by creating a random number between 0 and 100 and then places the object at 700,100 if the number is less than 50 and otherwise at 500,300. This means that each time you run the program, the object will have a 50/50 chance of being at either place. You will see shortly why we choose to put the object in one of two specific places instead of somewhere totally random.

8.9 Testing the Program

Enter the program and test it to verify that the RED object does appear in one of two places each time you run the program. Also notice that the phrase *Looking* appears at the bottom of the screen while the robot spins around looking for the object.

When the object is spotted, the phrase *Going To It* appears and the robot moves forward toward the object.

When it gets there, the phrase *Found It* appears and the program ends.

8.10 Enhancing the Program

Now it is time for you to try your hand at designing and implementing a task for the robot. Since this is your first big task, we want to help you get started.

The goal is to write a program that will allow the robot to find a RED object in a crowded room, that is, a room with other obstacles that can block the robot's vision and movements. From this chapter, you already know how to make the robot spin around in its current location to look for the object.

Chapter 4 showed you how to make the robot wander around a room and avoid the walls and obstacles. If you combine these two behaviors, the robot should be able to find a RED object in a crowded room.

The principle is easy to imagine. The robot should wander a bit, but not too long. When it stops, it should spin around and see if the object is in sight. If it is, it should try to go to it and if not, it should just wander a little more, etc. Figure 8.5 shows a main program that can perform these actions.

```
MainProgram:
  gosub Initialize
  Found=False
  repeat
    gosub RoamSome
    gosub LookForRed
  until Found
  xyString 10,580,"Found It"
end
```

Figure 8.5: This program searches a crowded room.

Notice that Figure 8.5 is similar to the **MainProgram** in Figure 8.4. The new program simply adds a call to a

RoamSome subroutine. It is your assignment to write this new module. Remember, it should make the robot move around the room just like it did in Chapter 4, but in your module it should only roam for a short period. Perhaps you could have it roam until it bumped into several objects. It might also be advantageous if the robot stopped sometimes before it actually bumped into something. Being out in the open when it starts to spin could give it a better chance of spotting the object. Of course, your module should also print a phrase at the bottom of the screen to let the user know what the robot is trying to do. This is especially important now that the robot is combining several actions to accomplish its goal, so add this line at the beginning of your module.

```
xyString 10,580,"Roaming "
```

```
Initialize:
  // create robot
  rLocate 50,50
  // make three objects
  rTurn -100-random(100)
  s=random(50)
  circle 200-s,300-s,400+s,350+s,Black,DarkGray
  s=random(50)
  rectangle 550-s,400-s,600+s,400+s,Black,DarkGray
  Line 300,100,600,200,50,DarkGray
  // create an object to find
  // choose from two places
  s=15
  if random(100)<50
    circle 700-s,100-s,700+s,100+s,RED,RED
  else
    circle 300-s,500-s,300+s,500+s,RED,RED
  endif
return
```

Figure 8.6: Use this new **Initialize** with your program.

Of course, your new program must have a different environment. The new **Initialize** module in Figure 8.6 creates three randomly sized obstacles for you. This is why we could not just place the RED object anywhere on the screen. We must make sure it does not overlap with one of these obstacles.

8.11 Summary

In this chapter you have learned:

❏ How `rLook()` and `rBeacon()` can provide limited vision capabilities for our robot.

❏ How the robot can be programmed to spin and look for an object of a specific color.

❏ How to make the robot move toward an object and decide if it successfully made it to its destination.

❏ How `xyString` provides more flexibility than `Print`.

❏ How several behaviors can be combined to make our robot more intelligent.

8.12 Exercises

Before moving on to the next chapter, test your knowledge and skill by trying the following exercises. Give each problem your best effort before reviewing the answers given in Appendix A.

1. Type in the programs described in the first part of this chapter and verify that the robot can find the RED circle and make its way to it (in an empty room).

2. Write the program described by section 8.10. Don't be discouraged if it takes more time than you expect. Programming can be challenging, but it is also very rewarding. When your programs don't work properly, see those problems as a game where you are challenged to track them down and correct them.

Chapter 9

Navigating a Maze

Nearly every robot club in existence has probably had a contest at one time or another to see if the members can build a robot that can navigate a maze. Sometimes the task is relatively easy because contestants know the maze specifications in advance. More advanced contests require the robot to navigate through an entirely unknown labyrinth, perhaps even learning from its mistakes so that it can run the maze perfectly on the second try.

This chapter will introduce you to some basic principles that will help you move a robot through a known maze. After mastering this material, you can learn about advanced maze navigation techniques from *Robot Programmer's Bonanza*.

9.1 Creating a Maze

The first thing we have to do is create a maze for our robot. The subroutine in Figure 9.1 will create the maze shown in Figure 9.2. Notice that the robot is also placed at the entrance to the maze.

All the statements present in Figure 9.1 have been used in previous programs, so you should be able to study the code and see how it works. The basic principle is simple. A gray rectangle is drawn, and lines of very wide widths are used to draw the maze pathways throughout the gray area. If anything is confusing, try commenting out a line that you do not understand and analyze the effect on the output screen. You might also insert SetColor commands at appropriate spots so you can see exactly what each graphic statement is doing.

```
InitMaze:
  LineWidth 10
  Rectangle 0,0,799,599
  rectangle 10,10,790,540,DarkGray,DarkGray
  LineWidth 95
  SetColor White
  Line 150,150,150,540
  Line  70,150,400,150
  LineTo 400,350
  Line 300,350,550,350
  Line 550,480,550,200
  Line 550,200,720,200
  Line 720,110,720,540
  rLocate 150,550
return
```

Figure 9.1: This subroutine creates a maze and places the robot at the entrance.

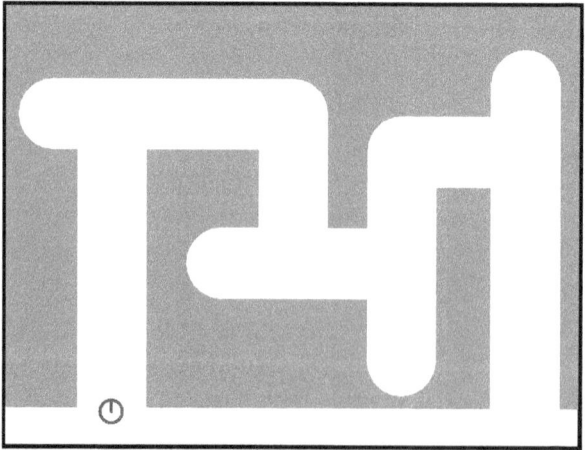

Figure 9.2: This maze is created by Figure 9.1.

9.2 Moving Into the Maze

Let's start by simply moving the robot into the maze. In fact, lets create code that will move the robot until it reaches the end of the first corridor. Let's assume our movement through the maze is controlled by a subroutine called **RunMaze**. The **MainProgram** for our system, along with the initial attempt at running the maze is shown in Figure 9.3.

```
MainProgram:
  gosub InitMaze
  gosub RunMaze
end

RunMaze:
  while rBumper()=0
    rForward 1
  wend
return
```

Figure 9.3: This program moves the robot into the maze.

If you run the program in Figure 9.3 (don't forget to add the `InitMaze` subroutine) you will see the robot move into the maze and follow the corridor until it reaches the far wall.

9.3 The `rFeel()` Function

The program in Figure 9.3, as with other programs in previous chapters, used the robot's bumpers to determine when it reached an object or in this case, the end of the corridor.

The bumpers have served us well so far, but it is time to introduce a more sophisticated sensor. In the real world bumpers are used usually only as fail-safe detectors. Generally, we would prefer a sensor that can "feel" obstacles blocking our path before actually bumping into them.

One way of doing this, on a real robot, is to shine an infrared light (invisible to humans) outward from the robot and then use an infrared detector to see if any of the light is reflected back. If none comes back, then we can be pretty sure there are no objects in the path.

We cannot be totally sure, because black objects might be able to absorb so much light that none or very little would be reflected back. Objects with unusual textures might not be seen either, because they could reflect most of the light off to the side instead of back toward the robot.

Most obstacles would be seen with this type of sensor though (as long as the objects are reasonably close to the robot), so they are common on many robots. The fact that they are not totally reliable is the reason a robot might also support bumpers as a fail-safe backup system.

Our simulated robot has five of these sensors mounted around the front perimeter of the robot at strategic positions (there are none on the back side of the robot). They can be read by the function rFeel(). If you replace the function rBumper() in Figure 9.3 with rFeel(), you will see that the robot moves down the corridor and stops a short distance from the wall, instead of bumping into it.

Since infrared light cannot be seen by humans, the robot appears to detect the walls almost by magic. Our inability to see infrared light can make it difficult for inexperienced programmers to debug robots that use infrared sensors. Fortunately, we are using a simulator so we can make it respond anyway we want.

There is a special version of rFeel() called rDFeel() that lets you see the area observed by the infrared sensors. When you use rDFeel() you should add a color as a parameter to tell rDFeel() what color should be used when displaying the observable areas. The chosen color will automatically be assumed to be invisible to the robot.

Substitute `rDFeel(RED)` in your program and run it again. This time you will see the location of all the sensors around the robot's perimeter. You will also see the robot stop when the front sensor reaches the far wall. After the robot senses the wall, it should back away a small amount to prevent the wall being sensed again. Recall that we had to do this with the bumpers too. We need to back up at least several pixels in this case though, because the distance that infrared light can be detected can vary considerably based on conditions such as the object's color and texture.

The codes for each of the sensors, starting with the back sensor and proceeding counter-clockwise around the robot are, 1, 2, 4, 8, and 16. Just as with the bumper sensors, each sensor represents one of the binary bits in the number returned by the function.

The `rDFeel()` function is much slower than `rFeel()`, so it generally should not be used unless you need to see what the robot is seeing, to help you debug the program.

9.4 Proceeding Through the Maze

When the robot stops, we know, by looking at the maze, that the robot should turn right and then at the next intersection it should turn right again and then left at the next junction.

We could tell the robot to turn right after it hit the first wall, then use another loop to find the next wall and then turn right again, then another loop to find the next wall, and so forth until the robot reaches the end of the maze.

By now though, you know you can just create one loop that finds the next wall and place it in a subroutine so that it can be called when needed. The code in Figure 9.4 shows how we could implement this principle to guide the robot through several turns in the maze.

Enter the code from Figure 9.4 (along with the other required routines and watch the robot move through the maze. When you have the program working, modify it so the robot makes it all the way through the entire maze.

```
RunMaze:
  gosub ForwardTillBlocked
  rTurn 90
  gosub ForwardTillBlocked
  rTurn 90
  gosub ForwardTillBlocked
  rTurn -90
  gosub ForwardTillBlocked
  rTurn -90
return

ForwardTillBlocked:
  while rFeel()=0
    rForward 1
  wend
  // back away from wall
  rForward -5
return
```

Figure 9.4: This code moves the robot through several turns of the maze.

9.5 Improving the Program

If you have successfully completed the above assignment, you will have a **RunMaze** subroutine that seems to perform the same general tasks over and over. The two tasks being performed repeatedly are:

Move to the next wall
Make the appropriate turn

It would be nice to put these two tasks inside a loop because the program would be much smaller. The problem, of course, is that the robot does not always make the same turn.

9.6 Array Variables

Fortunately, there is a solution. RobotBASIC supports a special type of variable known as an array.

An array is simply a *group* of variables that are assigned the *same* name. We can select the one we want from the group by indicating which one with a number called the *index*. Let's create a simple example to demonstrate how arrays work.

The command Dim A[5] creates (or *dimensions*) an array called **A** that can hold 5 different numbers. Similarly, the command Dim B[800] would create an array **B** that holds 800 numbers.

Let's work with the array **A** for the following examples. We know that **A** contains 5 different numbers, but they are no good to us unless we can choose which one we want to access. Imagine the five numbers are stored in 5 different envelopes that are labeled with the numbers from 0 to 4. When we want the number in envelope 0 (this would be called *element* 0), we ask for **A[0]**. Similarly, if we want the envelope labeled 3, we would ask for **A[3]**. The great thing about this, is that we can use a variable (like **x**) to specify which envelope we want (like this, **A[x]**).

The simple programs in Figure 9.5 show two examples that demonstrate how easily arrays can be used. Both examples assume that the array **A** has been dimensioned to hold 5 elements.

```
// example 1              // example 2
for i=1 to 3             for i=0 to 4
   A[i]=i*2                 print A[i]
next                     next
A[4]=50
A[0]=-5
```

Figure 9.5: These example programsdemonstrate how to use array variables.

Example 1 shows how we can give values to the array elements. We can certainly assign values directly as shown by the last two lines in the example. The `for` loop shows a more sophisticated way of assigning the elements (assuming the desired values can be calculated). The variable **i** will have a value of 1 the first time through the loop, then 2 and finally 3.

The first time through the loop, **A[1]** will be assigned a value of 2. The second time through the loop, **A[2]** will be assigned a value of 4 and finally, the third time through, **A[3]** will be 6. Study the code carefully to see how this happens.

Example 2 uses a loop to print the values of all 5 elements in the array. Notice that these same three lines (with minor changes to the `for` statement) could just as easily print all the elements in an array that holds thousands of elements. Utilizing these principles can make your programs more efficient.

It is important to know that an error will occur if you try to use an array element that has not yet been assigned a value (just as standard variables cannot be used until they have been assigned a value).

9.7 A Practical Example

Let's use the principles just discussed to improve the **RunMaze** subroutine shown in Figure 9.4. We know that we want the robot to turn 90°, then 90° again, then -90° and -90°.

We can create an array to hold these numbers and assign the values as shown in Figure 9.6. These statements would have to be performed before any of the array elements are used. A good place for these statements would be in the initialization subroutine.

```
Dim A[4]
A[0]=90
A[1]=90
A[2]=-90
A[3]=-90
```

Figure 9.6: These statements initialize the array.

Now that the array has been initialized, we can rewrite the **RunMaze** subroutine as shown in Figure 9.7.

```
RunMaze:
    for i=0 to 3
        gosub ForwardTillBlocked
        rTurn A[i]
    next
  return
```

Figure 9.7: A more efficient version of **RunMaze**.

Make these changes to the program and verify that the robot still performs properly. Once you have the program working, show you understand how to use arrays in this manner by modifying the program so that the robot completes the maze.

9.8 Real World Robots

When we tell our simulator to turn 90° it does exactly what we request. When we tell it to move forward, it does so in a perfectly straight line. Real robots do not respond so perfectly.

Real robots have friction so the wheels might not turn exactly as far as we expect, or the wheels might slip on the floor when they try to turn. These errors can cause havoc when we run programs that expect perfection from the robot they control.

RobotBASIC allows you to simulate the limitations of a real robot so you can determine how your programs can be modified to fix problems that could occur. If you place the command `rSlip 5` right after the `rLocate` statement in the initialization module, the robot will move as before, but each movement will have some random error (up to 5% in this case) added or subtracted from the desired movement.

If you make this change, and run the program again, you will see that it does not take long before the robot bumps into a side wall in the maze (use `rDFeel()` to see this happen if you wish). When this happens, the robot thinks it hit the end of the corridor (because **ForwardTillBlocked** just checks to see if ANY sensor has been triggered). Thinking it reached the end of the corridor causes the robot to start turning early, which aggravates the problems because the robot is now turning into side walls and making the wrong turns.

9.9 Correcting for Wheel Slip

We can correct the problems associated with wheel slip in this example by modifying the **ForwardTillBlocked** subroutine as shown in Figure 9.8.

```
ForwardTillBlocked:
  while (rFeel()&4) <> 4
    rForward 1
    if rFeel()=1 then rTurn -1
    if rFeel()=16 then rTurn 1
  wend
  // back away from wall
  rForward -5
return
```

Figure 9.8: This version of **ForwardTillBlocked** compensates for wheel slip.

The first change in Figure 9.8 is to have the `while` check the status of *only* the front sensor, which has a value of 4. This prevents the other sensors from affecting the loop's operation.

In order to examine *only* the front sensor, we have to perform a *binary and* (using the operator & as shown in Figure 9.8).

Remember, if more than one sensor is activated the number returned by `rFeel()` would be the *sum* of the sensors' positions so if 4 is activated and say 8 then the result would be 12. Now 12 is not equal to 4 and even though the front sensor is activated if we say `rFeel()<>4` then that is true since it is 12. But, this is misleading since we are trying to find out if the front sensor is activated or not and `rFeel() <> 4` does not give us the right information since it gives false even though we *might think* that it should give true. So we need to do something else.

The & serves to *mask* out the bits that we do not want so that they will become zero regardless of what they happen to be, and only keep the bit that we are interested in. So when we do `rFeel() & 4` we are forcing all bits in the number returned by `rFeel()` to become 0 except for the bit 4 (third bit) which is the bit for the front sensor. This bit will then be either 0 or 1 depending on if the front sensor is activated or not.

So by doing this masking using the & operator in the statement `while (rFeel() &4) <> 4` we are saying we only want to examine the front sensor bit and if that is not on then we keep inside the loop and if it is on then we get out of the loop. This works even if other sensors are also activated at the same time because we masked them out with the use of the `&4` action.

Next, the side sensors are checked (values 1 and 16). If the right sensor is triggered, the robot is asked to turn left. If the left sensor is triggered, a right turn is requested. Both of these turns are very small, just enough to send the robot back toward the middle of the corridor.

After making these changes run the program again and watch the robot correct itself as it encounters the side walls in the maze. It can be hard to see the small movements made by the robot, so here is a suggestion. Add the following lines to the initialization subroutine right after the rLocate statement. They allow the robot to leave a trail while moving as was discussed in Chapter 3 section 3.5.

```
LineWidth 2
rInvisible Green
rPen Down
```

If you want to compare the robot's path with the ideal robot, simply comment out the rSlip line and run the program again. The "real" robot's path is very different, but it still manages to find its way through the maze.

As you learn more about programming robots you will be able to make them deal with many real world situations.

9.10 Summary

In this chapter you have learned:

- ❑ How to use line and rectangle statements to draw a simple maze.
- ❑ How to move the robot down a corridor and detect the end of it.
- ❑ How rFeel() and rDFeel() can let you detect walls without touching them.
- ❑ How array variables can make programs more efficient.
- ❑ How RobotBASIC can simulate the random errors associated with real world robots.
- ❑ How sensors can be used to correct for the random errors associated with real world robots.

9.11 Exercises

Before moving on to the next chapter, test your knowledge and skill by trying the following exercises. Give each problem your best effort before reviewing the answers given in Appendix A.

1. Create the maze used in this chapter and make the robot move down the first corridor and stop at the end.

2. Modify the program in Exercise 1 so that the robot moves through several turns of the maze.

3. Modify the program in Exercise 2 so that array variables are used.

4. Create a program that moves the robot through the maze from start to finish.

5. Add slip to the program in Exercise 4 and use `rDFeel()` to see how errors occur.

6. Use the infrared sensors to correct the errors occurring in Exercise 5 as described in this chapter.

7. Modify your finished program so the robot begins at the exit of the maze. The robot should enter at the exit and proceed through the maze backward until it gets to the original entrance.

Chapter 10

Beacon Navigation

One of the things learned in Chapter 9 is that real robots do not behave perfectly. Friction, wheel slippage, and many other minor random conditions can prevent the robot from being exactly where we expect it to be. There are many potential solutions to this problem. This chapter will explore one possibility.

10.1 Celestial Navigation

Ships at sea, especially in the past, used the stars to pinpoint the boat's location. Sailors used a sextant to measure the angles to specific stars and then calculated the ship's position accordingly. If we place two or more beacons in the corners of a room we wish to navigate, we can calculate the robot's position relative to those beacons using similar methods.

10.2 What is a Beacon

A beacon can be anything the robot can locate and face. If your robot has a camera, you could use small disks of unusual colors for your beacons. If you have some electronic experience, you could create infrared light sources that pulse at a specific frequency.

You would also have to build a detector that could identify the frequency patterns associated with each of your beacons. This sounds complicated, but the principle is very common in electronic devices. Your TV remote control, for example, sends out pulses of infrared light that can be detected and identified by your television.

For our simulation, we will use two beacons composed of specific colors. Before we start writing a program to use the beacons though we need to explore some mathematical principles associated with this project.

Figure 10.1 shows a simulated room containing the robot. Beacons are located in the two left corners of the room. We will see later how the robot can determine the angles to each beacon (as indicated in the Figure).

Think of the room as the 4th quadrant of a graph. The upper wall of the room is the X axis and the left wall is the Y axis. This makes the upper left corner the origin with the coordinates of (0,0).

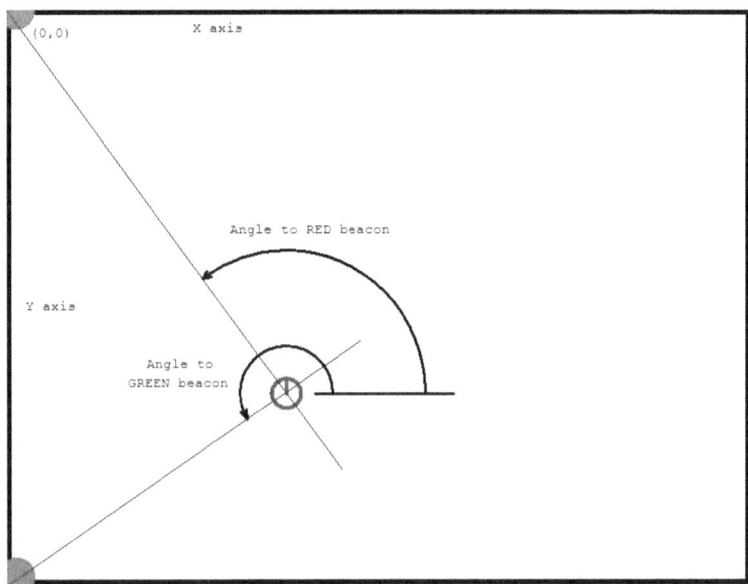

Figure 10.1: Two beacons can be seen in the left corners of this simulated room (Red up, Green down).

Notice the two lines in Figure 10.1 that start at the beacons and intersect at the robot's location. If we could find the **x,y** coordinates of the intersection of these line, we would know where the robot is located.

10.3 Math is Essential

If you are going to study robotics, engineering, or programming, you should take as many math classes as you can, as mathematics is the language of technology. If you find the following discussion difficult, just skim it and concentrate on the final formulas. As with many mathematical situations, the final formulas derived from a principle are all that is needed to implement programs based on that principle.

The equation for any straight line will take on the following form:

$$y = m*x + b$$

In the above equation, **m** is the slope of the line and **b** is the point where it intersects with the y-axis. This means that we can write the equations for both of the lines in Figure 10.1 as shown below. The letters **r** and **g** (for red and green) will identify the parameters for the lines for each beacon.

$$yr = mr*xr+br$$
$$yg = mg*xr+bg$$

The slope of a line can be defined as the amount of change in **y**, for some change in **x**. This principle, is also defined in trigonometry as the tangent of the angle of the line, relative to a horizontal base, which is how the angles are defined in Figure 10.1 We will define the angle for the line to the green beacon as **Ag** and the angle to the red beacon as **Ar**. This means the two slopes can be defined as below.

$$mr = tan(Ar)$$
$$mg = tan(Ag)$$

The two lines intercept the Y-axis at the corners of the room. Normally, these intersections should be stated in feet or inches, but in our simulation we will use pixels. This means **br** = 0 and **bg** = -599, although, at some point, we will want to think of these numbers in terms of feet and inches. Our room is 800 by 600 pixels, so if we assumed it was a reasonable size, perhaps 20 feet by 15 feet, we can calculate that a foot is 40 pixels and an inch is 3.3 pixels.

If we substitute all of these new values into the original equations for the lines, we get the following.

```
yr = tan(Ar)*xr
yg = tan(Ag)*xg-599
```

Remember, we want to find the point where these two lines intersect. At that point, **yr** will equal **yg** and **xr** will equal **xg**. Because of this, we will just refer to the intersection point as **x,y**. This means the equations can be rewritten for the intersection as follows.

```
y = tan(Ar)*x
y = tan(Ag)*x-599
```

Since the two equations are both equal to **y**, we can say that:

```
tan(Ar)*x = tan(Ag)*x-599
```

Solving the above equation for **x** gives:

```
x = 599/(tan(Ag)-tan(Ar)
```

Substituting the value of **x** back into the original equation for **yr** gives:

```
y = tan(Ar)*x
```

When everything is calculated, the above equation will result in a negative number because the robot is in the 4th quadrant of the graph. If we are going to use the number calculated for **y** to locate our robot, though, we will have to multiply it by -1 because the distances down the computer screen are positive. This gives us two final equations for the location of our robot as shown below.

```
x = 599/(tan(Ag)-tan(Ar)
y = -tan(Ar)*x
```

10.4 Using the Derived Equations

The equations derived in Section 10.3, allow us to find the location of our robot if we just know the angles from the robot to each of the beacons. Our next step is to develop a plan for finding these angles.

Let's assume we have some form of electronic compass on our robot. Such devices (with an accuracy of 5° or so) can actually be purchased for as little as $30 from companies like *Parallax*. More accurate devices can cost significantly more.

Our simulated robot has a simulated compass that can be accessed with the rCompass() function. The program in Figure 10.2 shows how to use this function and lets you see what values are provided as the robot rotates counter-clockwise.

```
rLocate 100,100
for i=1 to 10
  delay 2000
  print rCompass()
  rTurn -36
next
end
```

Figure 10.2: This program can help you understand the robots compass.

If you run the program and watch carefully as it executes, you'll discover a few important things. First, the robot assumes straight up (perhaps thought of as due North) to be zero degrees. It also assumes that the angles increase as the robot turns clockwise, which is the opposite of standard notations, which were the assumptions made when we derived our formulas. Fortunately, we can transform these numbers with minimal effort using mathematics.

If we obtain the angle provided by the compass, we can convert it to a counter-clockwise rotation by simply subtracting it from 360. We can move the direction for zero degrees to the right by subtracting 270. This means the correct angle can be calculated as shown below.

```
Angle = 360-rCompass()-270
```
or just
```
Angle = 90-rCompass()
```

If the new angle is negative we can make it positive by adding 360° like this.

```
if Angle<0 then Angle=Angle+360
```

We can put all this into subroutines that allows the robot to calculate the angles, and then the robot's **x,y** position on the screen (or, in a room if it was a real robot).

The subroutine **FindAngles** is shown in Figure 10.3. It is a bit longer than you might imagine, because each angle is actually found twice. Think about the beacons. They are not pinpoints of light so the robot will actually see the beacon before it turns directly towards the corner, which is a source of error.

If we find two angles to each beacon, approaching it from both clockwise and counter-clockwise directions, we can average those angles and get a more accurate answer.

Once **Ar** and **Ag** have been determined, the subroutine **FindXY** (see Figure 10.4) will utilize the formulas derived above to determine the probable position of the robot. **FindXY** also draws a vertical and horizontal line at the calculated position so you can see the accuracy of these routines.

```
FindAngles:
  // find them cclockwise first
  for a= 1 to 360
    if rBeacon(RED)
        Ar=90-rCompass()
        if Ar<0 then Ar=Ar+360
        break
    endif
    rTurn -1
  next
  for a= 1 to 360
    if rBeacon(GREEN)
        Ag=90-rCompass()
        if Ag<0 then Ag=Ag+360
        break
    endif
    rTurn -1
  next
  // save the angles
  TempAr=Ar
  TempAg=Ag
  //now find them clockwise
  for a= 1 to 360
    if rBeacon(RED)
        Ar=90-rCompass()
        if Ar<0 then Ar=Ar+360
        break
    endif
    rTurn 1
  next
  for a= 1 to 360
    if rBeacon(GREEN)
        Ag=90-rCompass()
        if Ag<0 then Ag=Ag+360
        break
    endif
    rTurn 1
  next
  // now average the angles
  Ar=(Ar+TempAr)/2
  Ag=(Ag+TempAg)/2
return
```

Figure 10.3: This subroutine determines the angles from the robot to the two beacons.

```
FindXY:
  mg=tan(DtoR(Ag))
  mr=tan(DtoR(Ar))
  rx=599/(mg-mr)
  ry=-mr*rx
  line rx,0,rx,600,3,LightBlue
  line 0,ry,800,ry,3,LightBlue
return
```

Figure 10.4: This subroutine uses the angles to each beacon to find the location of the robot.

If you combine Figures 10.3 and 10.4 with the **MainProgram** and **Initialization** module shown in Figure 10.5 you will have a program that moves the robot to 20 random locations and tests our equations by calculating where the program thinks the robot is. Furthermore, the program will compare the calculated positions to the actual positions and find the average error for the 20 tests.

Figure 10.6 shows the final output screen from the program. Notice that the cross-hairs indicate that the calculated position is relatively close to where the robot actually is. Notice also, that the average error was less than seven pixels, which would be about two inches in a 20 by 15 foot room. Many hobbyists would love to have a navigation system capable of pinpointing their robot to two inches.

10.5 Your Future in Robotics
The projects in this book only scratch the surface of the fantastic things available to you in the field of robotics. If you are truly interested in this field, plan to study subjects such as engineering, electronics, mathematics, physics, and programming. It will take a lot of work, but if this is something you enjoy, it will all be worth it.

```
MainProgram:
  xErr=0
  yErr=0
  for test=1 to 20
    gosub Initialization
    gosub FindAngles
    gosub FindXY
    xErr=xErr+abs(sx-rx)
    yErr=yErr+abs(sy-ry)
    delay 1000
  next
  xyString 200,10,"Ave x,y error = ",xErr/20,",",yErr/20
end

Initialization:
  LineWidth 6
  rectangle 2,2,797,597,Black,gray
  s=15
  c=Red\x=10\y=0
  circle x-s,y-s,x+s,y+s,c,c
  c=Green\y=590
  circle x-s,y-s,x+s,y+s,c,c
  sx=100+random(600)
  sy=100+random(450)
  rLocate sx,sy
return
```

Figure 10.5: These two modules complete the program described in this chapter.

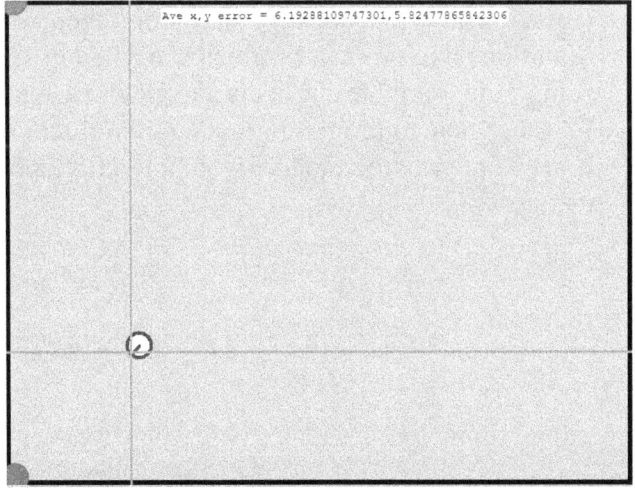

Figure 10.6: The program in this chapter produces this final output screen.

10.6 Summary

In this chapter you have learned:

- How beacons can be used to find the position of a robot in a room.
- Why mathematics is important in fields such as robotics.
- How trigonometry can be used to create a navigation system.
- What subjects you should study if you want a career in robotics.

10.7 Exercises

Before moving on to the next chapter, test your knowledge and skill by trying the following exercises. Give each problem your best effort before reviewing the answers given in Appendix A.

1. Enter the program described in this chapter and verify that it works as expected.

2. **FindAngles** subroutine is fairly long, and many parts of the code seem very similar to other parts. Situations like this can be greatly reduced in size by using array variables. This is a difficult assignment for those new to programming, but if you feel up to it, try to rewrite the module in a more efficient manner.

Chapter 11

Robotic Arms

Programming a robotic arm is very different from programming a mobile robot. This chapter will examine some fundamental requirements and principles associated with programming a robotic arm. Furthermore, it will provide a 3D robotic arm simulation that can be programmed like a real arm so that you can experiment with the concepts discussed here without the time and expense of building or buying a physical arm.

11.1 Real Robotic Arms

We cannot properly examine the programming aspects of a robotic arm, without considering potential hardware configurations. The maneuverability of a robotic arm is proportional to its degrees-of-freedom, which roughly translates to the number of joints that can be controlled. You could build an arm with only one or two degrees-of-freedom, but it would be difficult to accomplish anything practical with it. Even three degrees-of-freedom has many limitations (as we will soon see) but the limited motion greatly simplifies the mathematics needed for joint calculations making such an arm perfect for introducing fundamental ideas. For these reasons, we will concentrate on an arm with three degrees-of-freedom.

Don't be discouraged by the choice of a simplified arm. With a few compromises, such an arm can still perform interesting tasks while helping you learn the basic principles needed before moving on to more complicated systems.

Let's start by examining some decisions you might face when building an arm with three degrees-of-freedom. For the purposes of this chapter, we will assume the following movements as shown in Figure 11.1:
- A rotating base
- A shoulder joint attached to the base
- An elbow joint attached to the shoulder.

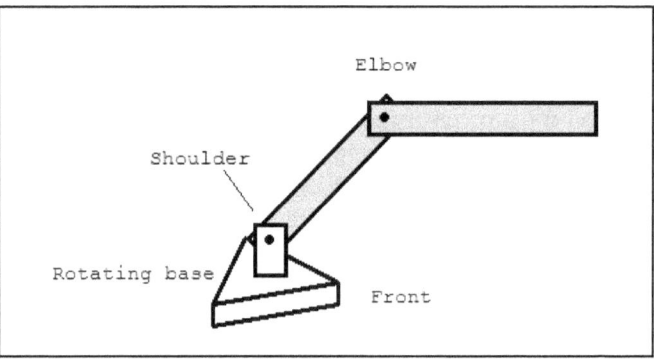

Figure 11.1: A simple arm with 3 degrees of freedom.

11.2 Choosing the Motors
With the configuration of the arm established, we need to decide on the types of motors to use. We will consider three motor types:
- Stepper motors
- DC gearhead motors
- Servomotors.
Each type has advantages and disadvantages.

Stepper motors do not require feedback, but they generally have limited torque and speed when compared to the other choices. Stepper motors are unique in that they draw the same amount of current when a joint is stationary as when it is moving so power requirements can be hefty. Stepper motors also require a specific sequence of pulses to control the motors movements but this is often accomplished with a stepper motor driver chip that provides both the logic and current drivers.

DC gearhead motors are generally the most powerful choice for a hobby arm, but they require some form of feedback such as a potentiometer, incremental encoder, or absolute encoder for each of the moveable joints. This complicates the process as your software will have to monitor the feedback to ensure proper movement. As with stepper motors, a driver chip is often the best way to power DC motors.

If you are building your first arm, hobby servomotors could be your best choice. They are composed of a DC motor and gear train, so they are very powerful for their size and weight. They also contain an integrated potentiometer and internal circuitry to automatically attain the commanded position. Again, a driver module is generally the easiest way to provide computer control of Servo motors.

11.3 Joint Options

Once you have chosen your motors, the next step is to decide how they will be mounted on your arm. You might be surprised at how the choices you make can affect the controlling software you need to write. The details of the mechanical assemblies are beyond the scope of this book but, as you will see, the mounting of these motors can affect how the arm moves and thus how it must be controlled.

The rotating base could be something as simple as a lazy-susan bearing with a motor mounted beneath the base. The shoulder joint is also relatively easy to implement because the motor can be mounted on the base with a direct drive to the joint. The placement of the motor for the elbow joint though, has at least two options. It is easy to imagine mounting the arm on the shoulder assembly itself (see Figure 11.2). If the motor is mounted this way, the angle of the elbow is measured from the shoulder assembly which means that any movement of the shoulder will alter the elbow angle relative to the base (but not to the shoulder).

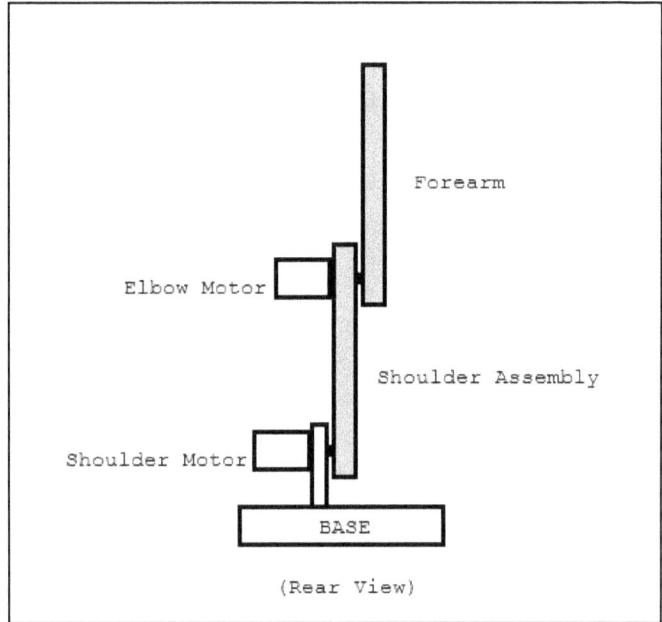

Figure 11.2: The elbow motor can be mounted on the shoulder assembly.

As an alternative, we could mount the elbow motor on the base and use a pulley system (see Figure 11.3) to move the elbow assembly. This has an obvious weight advantage because the shoulder motor does not have to lift the elbow motor in this configuration. Notice that in this case, the elbow assembly does not

move, relative to the base, when the shoulder is
moved.

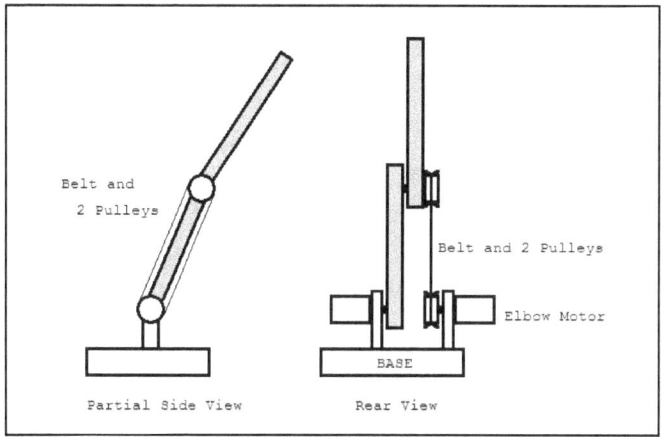

Figure 11.3: Moving the elbow motor to the base gives a
weight advantage.

11.4 End-effectors and Grippers

At the end of the elbow assembly (essentially a forearm)
our arm will need some form of end-effector to enable it to
pick up objects. This could be some form of hand with
finger-like grippers but that complicates the programming
problem immensely. In order for such an arm to perform
useful tasks (stacking blocks, for example) the end-effector
would need an additional three degrees of freedom so that
the hand can be oriented in relationship to the arm itself.
Since this complication is beyond the scope of this
introductory book we will use a simplified vacuum-based
gripper.

The basis for our end-effector will be a small 12-volt
vacuum cleaner used for shop work or small household
spills. Since we won't need much suction, you could even
make one from a box and a small fan. In either case a
small flexible hose should be connected to the vacuum
housing and run along the robotic arm to the gripper point

where it terminates in a brass or plastic tube connected to a wrist joint. As long as we keep the tube pointed downward, we could pick up small pieces of cardboard, serving as blocks to be manipulated, by switching the vacuum on.

Keeping the tube pointed downward could require another degree of freedom, as mentioned earlier, but not if we are creative. Remember how the elbow assembly can maintain its position relative to the base if the elbow motor is mounted on the base? We can do the same thing with the end-effector by using pulleys or even tie rods as shown in Figure 4. With this configuration the vacuum tube will always point downward regardless of the angles assumed by the elbow and shoulder.

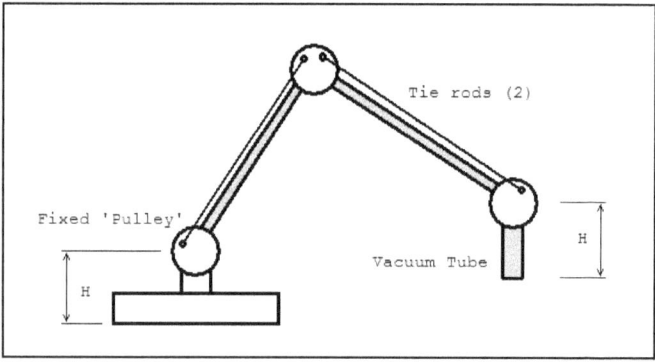

Figure 11.4: Pulleys or tie rods can maintain the orientation of the end-effector.

If we make the length of the vacuum nozzle the same as the height the arm is mounted above the base (H in Figure 11.4) then the mathematics for our arm become much easier. Many first-time arm builders fail to think about such considerations and end up building an arm that is too difficult to use.

11.5 Arm Mathematics

Let's look at some of the mathematical implications for our arm. The first thing we have to realize, is that if we wish to touch the end-effector to the floor, the angles **A** and **B** *must* always be the same, as shown in Figure 11.5. If **A** and **B** are not the same, then the bottom of the end-effector will mathematically be either above or below the working surface.

Notice in Figure 11.5 that when the arm is positioned with the gripper tube on the work surface, the elbow and shoulder assemblies form an equilateral triangle with the length (**L**) of the base of that triangle being the distance from the center of the arm's base to the center of the end-effector.

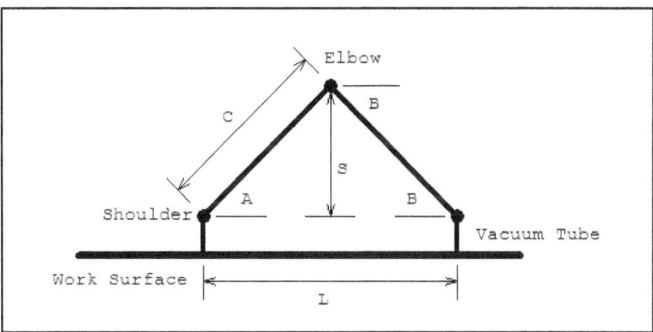

Figure 11.5: A little math can find the angles needed for positioning the arm.

If we know the value of **L**, we can calculate the angles **A** and **B** (which, remember, are always equal) using the following trigonometric equation.

$$A = \arctan(S/(L/2))$$

We still need the values for both **L** and **S** in order to calculate **A**. The value of **S** can be calculated using the Pythagorean Theorem as shown below.

$$S = \mathrm{Sqrt}(\ (L/2)*(L/2) + (C*C)\ )$$

This means we can determine the angles to use for the Shoulder and Elbow joints if we know the distance from the arm's base to our destination point (**L**). Normally the destination point for our arm would be in terms of an **X,Y** coordinate as shown in Figure 6. Notice we again have a right angle triangle so that the distance **L** can again be calculated using the Pythagorean Theorem. Also, in the same manner as before, we can calculate the angle of the base.

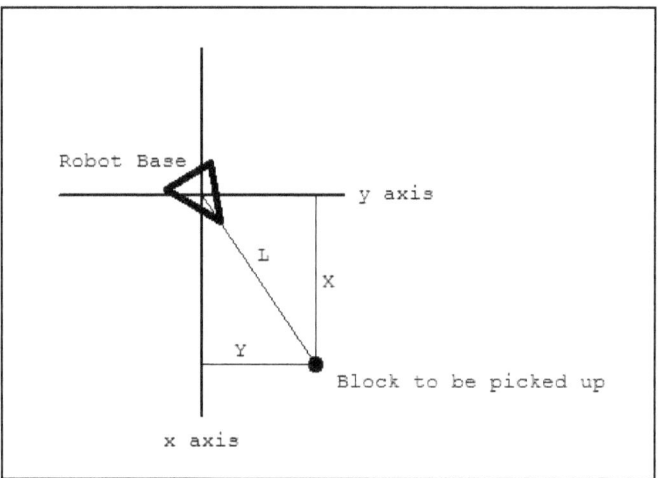

Figure 11.6: The rotational position of the base is also easy to calculate.

These calculations may seem complex, but they are easily implemented with the math functions in RobotBASIC. The important thing is that it is easy (at least for our simplified arm) to calculate the angles for the base, shoulder, and elbow needed for any **x,y** position on the working surface. Since our simplified model does not stack blocks to any appreciable height (the blocks are made of thin paper or cardboard) these calculations will work for isolated blocks or stacked blocks anywhere on the work surface.

The **x,y** positions of objects to be manipulated could be chosen manually, or from images from a web cam mounted above the work surface. RobotBASIC has vision commands that make it easy to import web cam images and calculate the positions of objects of specified colors within an image.

11.6 A Simulated Arm

We realize that you may want to experiment with an arm of this type, especially if you do not have to build or buy the arm. To that end we have implemented a simulation of a 3D arm identical in operation to the one described above. Figure 11.7 shows a screen shot of the simulated arm. In the simulation, the **x,y** coordinates of four locations have been manually specified.

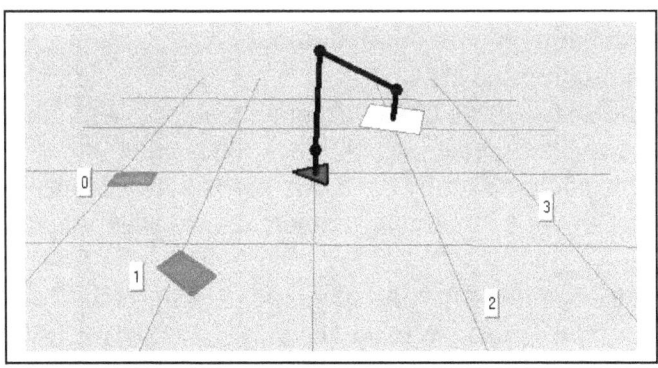

Figure 11.7: This 3D simulated arm was written with RobotBASIC.

Normally, if we are programming a real arm there will be significant changes to the code depending on the types of motors and sensors used for the construction. One solution to such a problem is to isolate all the motor related commands to a single module. Let's see how that might work.

Assume we have a subroutine called **MoveArm** that performs the task of moving the arm based on the value of three variables: **Base**, **Elbow**, and **Shoulder**. If any of these variables contains a zero, then that joint will not move when the subroutine is called. If one or more of these variables contains a number, such as 1 or -1, then the associated joint will move that many degrees (in this case one degree) either forward or backward depending on the sign of the number.

Furthermore, we will assume the **MoveArm** subroutine somehow reads sensors (in the case of DC motors) or keeps track of the current joint positions (for stepper or servomotors) and places the current angle for each joint in the variables **ElbowAngle** and **ShoulderAngle**. Changing one line of code in the simulation lets it emulate how the elbow motor is mounted (as discussed earlier) so you can experiment with both configurations.

The subroutine **MoveArm** also assumes the variable **InHand** is zero if no object is being held, or is a number from 1 to 3 to indicate which block the hand holds. This variable could be set by code that keeps track of where the objects are, or by analyzing camera data as mentioned earlier.

Before calling **MoveArm**, your code can set the variable **Vac** to **true** or **false** to make the arm pickup or release objects (the simulator won't let you release an object unless the end-effecter is near the work surface).

As stated earlier, the details of how this subroutine operates for a real arm will depend on the motors used as well as the type of ports and the buffering circuitry. Since this article is about programming the arm itself, not about building a motor interface, we will assume the subroutine **MoveArm** already exists. This works out perfectly for our simulated arm because we provide a **MoveArm** subroutine that works exactly as described above.

Notice the power of the above principle. Using this strategy, anyone can learn how to program an arm no matter what motors it might eventually use or even if it never exists at all. Then later, if a real arm becomes available, all the same code can be used with it if an appropriate **MoveArm** is written.

11.7 Programming the Arm

We encourage you to program the arm to perform simple tasks such as picking up blocks and moving them to predetermined locations, as these are tasks that represent an appropriate level of difficulty at this stage in your progress.

We also realize that some readers will want a project with more rigor, and we would like to oblige. All we need is an interesting application – something complex enough to be fun and challenging, but yet not too complex, since this is an introductory text. After careful thought, this is the chosen application.

The arm will be able to move or stack three different colored sheets of paper at four specific places in the work area. The human interface with the arm will consist of a series of buttons as shown in Figure 8.

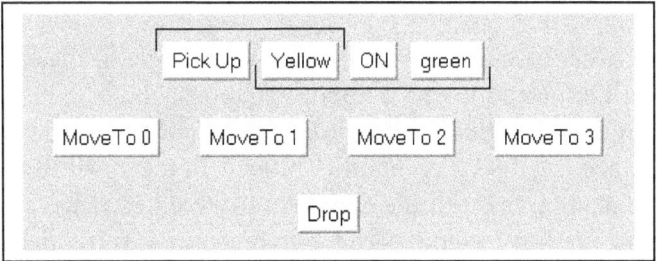

Figure 11.8: These buttons provide the human interface to control the arm.

Using the buttons the user will be able to move the arm to one of the four positions and pick up or drop a paper block. The user can also request more complex actions such as PICKUP GREEN or even something relative complicated such as putting the YELLOW ON RED.

In the above examples, we will want the arm to demonstrate a reasonable amount of intelligence. The arm, for example, should ignore a request to DROP a block if it is not holding one. Even in complex situations the arm should try its best to achieve the requested goal. If, for example, you ask it to place the YELLOW block on the RED block, it should first clear any blocks that may already be on the RED block, placing them at some temporary positions. It should then pick up the YELLOW block, automatically discarding any blocks that might be stacked on it, and finally drop the YELLOW block on the RED block.

The program we are going to write will perform all of the above functions and more, but it will not necessarily carry out its orders in the most efficient manner because we will use simplifications when possible. These simplifications will ensure that the code will be easy to write and understand, even for beginners. Once you see how the code works, we encourage you to modify it in ways that eliminate some of the idiosyncrasies created by our simplifications.

In order to make it easy to follow the logic of the code, we will explore it using a top down approach. The most complicated routine of our system is certainly the one that can place any block on another block. In the spirit of top-down design, this routine can be easily created if we assume we have modules that can perform specific tasks for us. The code to implement this **ColorOnColor** subroutine is shown in Figure 11.9.

The routine assumes that the human interface portion of our code will put the source color (**Yellow** in Figure 11.8) in the variable **curcol1** and the destination color (**green** in Figure 11.8) in the variable **curcol2**. Notice how easy it is to implement this complicated routine if we assume we have modules that can do the work for us.

The first thing this routine needs to do is remove any blocks that may be on top of the destination color. We can easily clear away all the blocks by simply picking up the destination color and then dropping it. This means that our assumed subroutine **PickUpColor** must perform all that is necessary to pick up the block whose color is held in the variable **block** including the discarding of any blocks piled on it. The **Drop** routine will simply put the block currently held by the hand, down at the current arm position.

```
ColorOnColor:
   // places color curcol1 ON curcol2
   block = curcol2  // clear destination block
   gosub PickUpColor
   gosub Drop
   block = curcol1
   gosub PickUpColor  // get the block to stack
   block = curcol2
   gosub MoveOver
   gosub Drop
return
```

Figure 11.9: This routine completes a complicated task by letting other modules do most of the work.

The next thing this routine needs to do is pick up the source block, specified by **curcol2**. It can do this easily by using the **PickUpColor** routine again. Next a new routine, **MoveOver**, will move the arm to the position of the block specified by the variable **block**. At this point, the arm is holding the source block and is currently positioned over a cleared destination block so all we have to do is call **Drop** again.

The power of this simplicity should not be taken lightly. Our **ColorOnColor** routine operates much like the executive of a large corporation who makes decisions about what needs to be done, but relies on the expertise of appropriate managers and workers to carry out the tasks. All of the actual work performed in the **ColorOnColor** routine is handled by subordinate subroutines. Of course, we must build those routines too, and if they are complicated we will assume there are even more subordinate routines to provide additional help.

The **MoveArm** subroutine, mentioned earlier, will reside at the lowest level of our hierarchal structure of subroutines and directly control the hardware. None of the upper-level routines will access the hardware at all. This means you can easily utilize most of the code designed for this project with any arm you might build regardless of what type of motors you want to use by simply writing your own **MoveArm** routine.

This principle allowed us to create a **MoveArm** for our simulated arm so that you can experiment with our code or write totally new routines of your own, without the need for a physical arm. You can download the complete demonstration software discussed in this chapter and the full source code for the simulated arm from our web page, as it is too long to print here.

11.8 Summary
In this chapter you have learned:
- ❑ The fundamental principles of building a real robotic arm.
- ❑ About the different types of motors that can be used when building an arm.
- ❑ How different joint configurations can affect how an arm moves.
- ❑ That an arm's end-effector can take various forms.
- ❑ Why an understanding of mathematics is an essential aspect of programming a robotic arm.

❑ About a simulated arm that can be programmed just like a real physical arm.

11.9 Exercises

Before moving on to the next chapter, test your knowledge and skill by trying the following exercises. Give each problem your best effort before reviewing the answers given in Appendix A.

1. Download and run the demo program from our web site and watch the YouTube video discussing the simulated arm. Discuss your impressions of how the arm is able to carry out your instructions.

2. Program the simulated arm to pick up a single piece of paper from a known position and deposit it at another predetermined position.

3. Assuming you know where all the pieces of paper are in the arm simulation, program the arm to stack all the pieces in the empty position.

Chapter 12

Walking Robots

The long-range goal for many robot hobbyists is the development of a humanoid robot, especially a walking humanoid. The good news is there are many humanoid robots available, both as kits and assembled units. The bad news is that most of the robots available, especially those with reasonable prices, are not truly suitable for learning about robotic walking algorithms.

12.1 Programming with Poses

The software that comes with many humanoid robots lets the user "program" the robot by creating a variety of *poses* and then linking those poses together in an appropriate sequence to create lifelike motions. This methodology has the advantage of allowing nearly anyone to quickly create custom demonstrations, such as walking or dancing, that make the robot *appear* to have some degree of intelligence. Unfortunately, robots programmed in this way are far less capable than they seem.

Robots that walk using a sequence of poses, for example, often cannot handle even simple problems such as gentle inclines or uneven terrain, let alone steep grades or stairways. Robots capable of dealing with those situations require more sensors than you find on the humanoid robots currently aimed at the hobbyist market. In many cases, the only sensory information available from a walking robot is the angle of each of the joints.

12.2 Minimal Requirements

At the very least, a proper walking robot must know the location of its limbs, when it is falling, the direction of the fall, and when each foot makes contact with the ground. Based on our experimentation, this sensor information is the bare minimum needed to create a walking algorithm.

In order to experiment with walking algorithms, a simple walking robot simulator was developed using RobotBASIC because of its ability to create flicker-free animation. Figure 12.1 shows the humanoid figure created by the simulation. A major goal for the simulator was to maintain simplicity so that programmers new to walking algorithms could be productive with a reasonable amount of effort. Because of that, some compromises had to be made.

Figure 12.1: A simulation of a walking humanoid robot

12.3 Compromises

One of the major compromises made, is that the simulated figure is only two-dimensional. This means it can fall forward and backward but not side-to-side. While this may seem like a major limitation in the simulation it actually represents a huge advantage because it greatly reduces the complexities that have to be mastered by the programmer. From an educational point of view, the user can learn how to deal with balancing the robot without being overwhelmed with too many parameters that greatly complicate the programming.

Another compromise that was made is that the robot will fall (when off balance) at a steady pace, rather than continually accelerating as it falls. This was deemed acceptable because the robot must catch itself early in the fall anyway, meaning that it should never fall far enough for acceleration to have any significant effects.

12.4 Sensors

When programming the simulation, you will have access to the data from a variety of sensors, including the angle of each joint, the ability to know when a foot touches the ground, and tilt information. All sensors in our simulation will have some limitations, but again, the compromises chosen should make it easier to use the simulator for learning about the fundamental aspects of walking.

Since the full source code for the simulator can be downloaded, you can study the code and modify everything to meet your specific interests. In addition to being able to modify the robot and its environment, this also means you can add and explore the value of additional sensors should you wish to investigate alternative approaches.

12.5 Controlling the Joints

At the lowest level of control, you can move each joint (as you might with a stepper or servo motor). To speed the learning process though, numerous mid-level subroutines have been provided that move the joints and body in predetermined ways, and you can always add more of your own. For example there is a subroutine called **LtLegForward** that moves the left leg forward while maintaining the calf angle with the thigh. The subroutine **LtThighForward** moves the leg, but maintains the calf angle with the horizon. Let's see how each of these can be used and how the robot responds.

Look at the code fragment in Figure 12.2. The **Init** subroutine initializes the simulated robot and makes it ready to receive action commands. The `for` loop moves the robot from the position in Figure 12.3A to that of Figure 12.3B. If we change the subroutine call in Figure 12.2 from **LtLegForward** to **LtThighForward**, the robot will move from position A to position C.

```
gosub Init
for a=1 to 15
   gosub LtLegForward
   gosub DrawRobot
next
```

Figure 12.2: This code moves the robot's left leg
(see Figure 12.3B).

12.6 The DrawRobot Subroutine

At the end of the `for` loop in Figure 12.2, there is a call to **DrawRobot**. This subroutine actually performs all the necessary calculations and draws the robot in the new position. It also updates all the sensory data. The movement is very smooth since the simulation goes through many intermediate positions (15 in this example) before reaching its destination. The call to **DrawRobot** could have been placed inside the movement routines (such as **LtLegForward**) but when we ask the robot to move several joints at once (more on this in a moment) it is much more efficient to wait till all angles have been modified before drawing the robot in its new position.

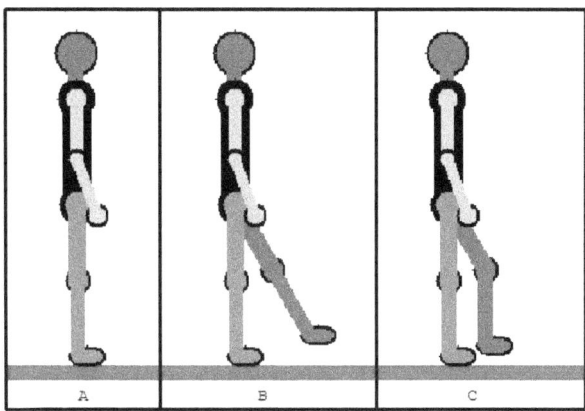

Figure 12.3: A-Starting position, B-Left leg forward, C-Left thigh forward

12.7 Moving Several Joints Simultaneously

As just mentioned, sometimes we will want to move several joints at once. Look at the code in Figure 12.4. The first `for` loop prepares to walk by raising the left leg and leaning the body forward. The second loop continues raising the left leg while moving the right leg backward (effectively moving the body forward since the body is supported by the right foot).

Notice in Figure 12.4, how both arms are moved in a natural motion while the other movements are occurring. The humanoid ends up as shown in Figure 12.5 by the end of the second loop.

```
gosub Init
for a=1 to 15
   gosub LtThighForward
   gosub BodyForward
next
for a=1 to 10
   gosub LtThighForward
   gosub RtArmForward
   gosub LtArmBackward
   gosub RtLegBackward
   gosub DrawMan
next
for a=1 to 40
   gosub DrawMan
next
```

Figure 12.4: This code starts the robot moving in a walking motion.

Figure 12.5: The code in Figure 12.4 produces this position.

12.8 The Robot Can Fall

There is a third loop in Figure 12.4 that appears to do nothing other than draw the robot. If you run the program though, you will notice that once the robot reaches the position shown in Figure 12.5 it will be off balance and continued calls to the **DrawRobot** subroutine will cause it to fall with the left foot as the pivot point. Once the right foot hits the ground, it *automatically* becomes the new pivot point and the robot will either be balanced or it will start to fall around the right foot.

12.9 Finding the Balance Point

This is another compromise in the design of the simulator. The most forward foot that is on the ground is always considered as the balancing point for the figure. As long as the robot is walking forward this is not an unreasonable compromise. If the robot starts to fall though, it can sometimes create an awkward movement of the limbs, but at least it is easy to see when your program is not keeping the robot properly balanced.

> **Note:** The **Init** subroutine chooses the right foot as the initial balance point.

Once the robot has reached the position shown in Figure 12.5 it needs to put its left foot on the ground. If it does nothing, it will fall forward (which will bring the foot to the ground, but may create a significant imbalance because the body will move forward too). Alternatively, the figure can start straightening the left leg, or perhaps bending the right leg. All of these actions will eventually cause the right foot to reach the ground. Some of these options could work better going up hill; others might be preferred when going down a slope. One of the great things about using a simulator is that you can easily play with all the options and determine appropriate ways for your robot to move, but without the possibility of damaging it if your programs do not work.

12.10 Autonomous Decisions

Programming the robot for autonomous walking however, is harder than you might imagine. If you choose to make the robot straighten its left leg, for example, you can't just tell it to straighten its left leg because you have no idea where the ground is in relation to the foot. One solution is to straighten the leg *until* the foot touches the ground (or until it becomes fully extended). The code in Figure 12.6 shows one way of accomplishing this, since the subroutine **LtLegStraighten** generates no action if the leg is already straight.

```
repeat
  gosub LtLegStraighten
  gosub DrawRobot
until MainFoot=Lt
```

Figure 12.6: This code continues until the left foot touches the ground.

Checking the value of the variable **MainFoot** is how the programmer can determine when the left foot has reached the ground. In addition to knowing which foot is the balance point, the programmer needs to know if the robot is falling, either forward or backward. This can be done in the simulation by testing the variable **Tilt** to see which of the following predefined constants it currently matches.

Constant	Meaning
Forward	The robot is off balance and falling forward.
Backward	The robot is off balance and falling backward.
Vertical	The robot is near vertical (and balanced).
Balanced	The robot is forward but still balanced.

If the robot is falling backwards, the code fragment in Figure 12.7 shows how you can direct it to try to regain its balance. It is important to realize that there is no guarantee that this code will work. The simulator has been designed so that the robot's movements are slightly faster than the fall rate, but if the robot is significantly off balance, then it may not be able to recover. Situations like this can be avoided by not letting the robot get too far out of balance. This can be done by having the program constantly monitor the variable **Tilt** and make appropriate adjustments by moving the robot's body forward and backward during the walking motion.

```
while Tilt=Backwards
    gosub BodyForward
wend
```

Figure 12.7: This code fragment tries to keep the robot from falling backwards.

12.11 Maintaining Balance

Maintaining proper balance while walking is not an easy task. This is especially true, because the robot may be balanced when it steps off on the left foot but be totally out of balance as soon as its weight is transferred to the right foot (when the right foot becomes the new balance point). The only way to prevent this is to maintain proper body orientation during all movements. Also, even if you derive an algorithm that works on level ground, expect failure when the robot encounters a slope.

Learning how to create an algorithm that allows the robot to react to uneven terrain all by itself can be challenging and time consuming, but also very rewarding. The feeling of success you get when the simulated robot takes a few steps on its own can be just as satisfying as programming the real thing.

12.12 A YouTube Video

If you would like to see the simulation in action before you try any programming, you can visit our web page (www.RobotBASIC.com) or just search YouTube for **RobotBASIC Walking Humanoid** and watch a short video showing the concepts discussed here, in action. The video concludes with the demonstration of a simple algorithm that allows the robot to autonomously handle a wide variety of uneven terrains.

The algorithm is based on the idea that an autonomous robot has to repeat left and right steps as shown by the code in Figure 12.8. In order to perform properly, the **LtStep** and **RtStep** subroutines must keep the robot balanced while constantly adjusting the leg angles to handle unknown slopes.

Additionally, each of these routines must terminate with the robot returning to a predetermined *normalized* position so that the next step starts from a known condition. Without this normalized position, even small errors will add up over time and cause an imbalance that cannot be corrected. The **StartWalk** routine should move the robot to the normalized position while the **StopWalk** must find a balanced standing position.

Our version of all these routines are provided, but it is suggested you try to write your own before scrutinizing or improving on ours. .

```
gosub Init
gosub StartWalk
repeat
  gosub LtStep
  gosub RtStep
until AcrossScreen
gosub StopWalk
```

Figure 12.8: This code makes the robot walk across the screen, but only if you have the proper subroutines.

12.13 Summary
In this chapter you have learned:
- How a walking robot simulator can help you learn how to program a humanoid robot.
- The basic movements necessary to begin a walking motion.
- What sensors are necessary for autonomous walking.
- The basic principles for navigating uneven terrain and keeping the robot balanced.

12.14 Exercises
Before moving on to the next chapter, test your knowledge and skill by trying the following exercises. Give each problem your best effort before reviewing the answers given in Appendix A.

1. Watch the video and run the downloadable demo available on our web page to see the robot in action.

2. Develop your own algorithm for making the robot complete a single step on level ground.

3. Develop your own algorithm for making the robot take several steps on level ground.

4. Develop your own algorithm for making the robot handle an up *or* down slope of a fixed incline.

5. Develop your own algorithm for autonomous walking over uneven terrain.

6. Examine the demo program and discuss the algorithm used.

Appendix A

Solutions to Exercises

The solutions for most of the exercises in the book will be shown and explained in this Appendix. Remember, these are just *Example* solutions and are not necessarily the only way to solve the exercises.

The solutions for each chapter start on a new page to make them easy to locate.

Solutions: Chapter 1

Solution for challenge in Section 1.8

```
SetColor RED
LineWidth 3
Line 0,0,799,599
SetColor Green
LineWidth 20
Line 799,0,100,400
SetColor Blue
LineWidth 5
Line 400,300,799,300
End
```

Solution for challenge in Section 1.9

The dimension given in Figure 1.6 help you in determining the coordinates (x,y) of the points required to define the rectangle and the triangle.

For the rectangle:

Top left corner $x = 400$ $y = 300$

Bottom right corner $x = 700$ $y = 500$

For the triangle:

1st vertex (top left) $x = 100$ $y = 100$

2nd vertex (bottom right) $x = 400$ $y = 200$

3rd vertex (bottom left) $x = 100$ $y = 300$

Also as indicated we need the line width to be set to 3. So now we can derive the program as:

```
linewidth 3
rectangle 400,300,700,500,blue
line 100,100,400,200,3,blue
lineto 100,300,3,blue
lineto 100,100,3,blue
```

Solution for challenge in Section 1.10

Remember that the `rSpeed` command will cause the robot to be slower when it is given a bigger the number and vice versa.

```
rLocate 100,200
rTurn 90
rspeed 220    //make it go slowly
rForward 500
rTurn 180
rspeed 0      //make it go fastest
rForward 500
End
```

Solution for Exercise 1.1

```
rlocate 20,20
rturn 90
rforward 760
rturn 90
rforward 560
rturn 90
rforward 760
rturn 90
rforward 560
```

Solution for Exercise 1.2

To make the robot go diagonally from top left corner to bottom right corner we need to place the robot at position (20,20) then turn the robot to face the bottom right corner then forward the distance required. You could use math (the Pythagorean Theorem) to determine these values, but for now, just experiment to find the required values for the turn direction and the distance. Appropriate values are shown below.

```
rlocate 20,20
rturn 126
distance = 939
rforward distance
rturn 180
rforward distance
```

Solutions: Chapter 2

Solution for Challenge in Section 2.4

The changes to make the program draw squares will have to be done for *each* line in the program. Lots of work! You also have to do some addition to get the correct value for the y-coordinate. The code listed below lets RobotBASIC to do the math.

```
LineWidth 3
Rectangle 100,100,350,100+250
Rectangle 400,100,650,100+250
Rectangle 400,350,650,350+250
Rectangle 100,350,350,350+250
End
```

Solution for Challenge in Section 2.7

See solution for Exercise 2.5 below.

Solution for Exercise 2.1

```
LineWidth 3
Rectangle 100,100,350,200,red,red
Rectangle 400,100,650,200,blue,blue
Rectangle 400,350,650,450,yellow,yellow
Rectangle 100,350,350,450,brown,brown
End
```

Solution for Exercise 2.2

```
width = 250
height = 100
x = 100
y = 100
linewidth 5
Rectangle x,y,x+width,y+height
x = 400
linewidth 8
Rectangle x,y,x+width,y+height
y = 350
linewidth 3
Rectangle x,y,x+width,y+height
x = 100
linewidth 15
Rectangle x,y,x+width,y+height
End
```

Solution for Exercise 2.3

In this exercise the idea is for you to realize the advantage of having variables instead of numbers. Using variables you can just change one line of code to change many places in the program wherever the variable is being used. So notice how much easier it was to do the modification in the second version than in the first version.

```
//had to change every line and figure out
//the value by adding
LineWidth 3
Rectangle 100,100,200,200
Rectangle 400,100,500,200
Rectangle 400,350,500,450
Rectangle 100,350,200,450
End
```

Now for the easy way.

```
//easy just one change
LineWidth 3
width = 100   //just here
height = 100
x = 100
y = 100
Rectangle x,y,x+width,y+height
x = 400
Rectangle x,y,x+width,y+height
y = 350
Rectangle x,y,x+width,y+height
x = 100
Rectangle x,y,x+width,y+height
End
```

Solution for Exercise 2.4

```
//need to get X,Y
Print "This program will draw four
rectangles."
Print "It will allow you to specify the
width and height."
Print "it will also allow you to specify
the x,y position"
print "   of the top left corner of the
last drawn rectangle"
Input "Enter Width", width
Input "Enter Height", height
Input "Enter X value",X  //capital X
Input "Enter Y value",Y  //capital Y
x = 100
y = 100
Rectangle x,y,x+width,y+height
x = 400
Rectangle x,y,x+width,y+height
y = 350
Rectangle x,y,x+width,y+height
x = 100
//notice using Capital X and Y
Rectangle X,Y,X+width,Y+height
End
```

Solution for Exercise 2.5

Here is a suggested path. Notice how the code lets RobotBASIC do the math work. The number 20 is used to make sure the robot stays 20 pixels away from the walls. This is because the robot has a radius of 20 pixels. This will ensure the robot does not crash into the walls.

```
LineWidth 3
Rectangle 200,400,500,550
Circle 200,200,400,300
Line 400,100,700,500
rLocate 350,350
// Enter your code here
  rturn -90
  rforward 200
  rturn 90
  rforward 350-20
  rturn 90
  rforward 800-20-150
End
```

Solutions: Chapter 3

Solutions for the challenges in Section 3.5

- You need the number to be 360 since there are 360° in a circle.
- You need to change the numbers for the `rForward` and/or `rTurn` so that they are bigger. Try changing one then the other then both to see what effects you get.

Solutions for Exercise 3.1

- Read chapters 1 to 5 (`For` loop)
- Keep reading until you reach chapter 5 (`Repeat` loop)
- While you have not yet reached chapter 5 keep reading (`while` loop)

Solutions for Exercise 3.3

Change the statement `Until b=1` to `Until b=2`.

Solutions for Exercise 3.4

In Figure 3.5 we used `while b=0`. This means that as soon as b is not zero we get out of the loop. So either button would cause that since either 1 or 2 is not 0.

In Figure 3.6 we used `Until b=1` which means that the loop will only stop when b equals 1 and that only happens if the left button is pushed. Also see the solution for Exercise 3.3 above.

Solutions: Chapter 4

Solution for Exercise 4.2
Here is a suggested program

```
rLocate 400,300
while True
    // move till bumped
    while rBumper()=0
        rForward 1
    wend
    // now turn away
    if rBumper()=4
        rTurn 150+random (61)
    elseif rBumper()=2
        rTurn -90
    elseif rBumper()=8
        rTurn 90
    elseif rBumper()=6
        rTurn -270
    elseif rBumper()=12
        rTurn 270
    endif
    rForward 1
wend
end
```

Solution for Exercise 4.2
Add these lines right after the rLocate statement.
```
LineWidth 4
Circle 150,200,300,300,Blue,Red
Rectangle 450,300,600,500,Red,Blue
```

Solution for Exercise 4.2
Instead of 90 or -90 and 270 and -270 try

      `90 + random(20)` or `-(90+random(20))`

And

      `200+random(80)` or `-(200+random(80))`

Also you may want to try `random(81)` instead of `random(61)`. But in any case try different values.

Solutions: Chapter 5

Solution for Exercise 5.2
See the solution for Exercise 4.2 and also add these lines
```
Circle 50,50,150,80,DarkGray,DarkGray
Circle 80,70,110,180,DarkGray,DarkGray
```

Solutions: Chapter 6

Solution for Exercise 6.2

In the **CheckMouse** subroutine in Figure 6.2 change the line that says

```
if b=0 then return
```

to

```
if b<> 1 then return
```

Do you know why this works?

Solution for Exercise 6.3

In the **Initialization** subroutine in Figure 6.2 change the line that says

```
s = 15 //size of objects
```

to

```
s = 40 //size of objects
```

Solution for Exercise 6.4

In the **Initialization** subroutine in Figure 6.2 after the line that says

```
s = 15 //size of objects
```

Add this line

```
sq = 40 //size square object
```

Then in the **DrawSquare** and **EraseSquare** subroutines in Figure 6.3 change all the +s or -s to +sq or -sq

Solution for Exercise 6.5

In the **MainProgram** in Figure 6.1 change the if-blocks to

```
if Selected=1
    gosub MoveCircle
    gosub DrawSquare
elseif Selected=2
    gosub MoveSquare
    gosub DrawCircle
endif
```

Solution for Exercise 6.6

Try this program

```
MainProgram:
  rLocate 400,300
  while true
     gosub MoveUntillBumped
     gosub TurnAway
  wend
End

MoveUntillBumped:
   while rBumper()=0
      readmouse x,y,b
      if b = 1
         rForward 1
         rTurn -1
      elseif b = 2
         rForward 1
         rTurn 1
      else
         rForward 1
      endif
   wend
Return

TurnAway:
   if rBumper()=4
      rTurn 150+random (61)
   elseif rBumper()=2
      rTurn -90
   elseif rBumper()=8
      rTurn 90
   elseif rBumper()=6
      rTurn -270
   elseif rBumper()=12
      rTurn 270
   endif
   rForward 1
Return
```

Solutions: Chapter 7

Solution for Exercise 7.2

Change the **Initialization** subroutine in Figure 7.1 to

```
Initialization:
  LineWidth 10
  SetColor GREEN
  Line 100,500,100,400
  LineTo 120,300
  LineTo 140,250
  LineTo 160,175,10,white
  LineTo 180,150
  LineTo 200,130
  LineTo 225,120
  LineTo 250,100
  LineTo 300,90,10,white
  LineTo 350,110
  LineTo 450,90
  LineTo 600,200
  LineTo 500,330
  LineTo 600,450,10,white
  LineTo 550,500
  LineTo 350,550
  LineTo 100,500
  rLocate 100,500
  rInvisible GREEN
return
```

and see what happens.

Solution for Exercise 7.3

Change the line in the **Initialization** subroutine in Figure 7.1 that says

```
LineWidth 10
```

To

```
LineWidth 4
```

Also add the line

```
LT = 0
```

Just before the `return` as we did in the chapter.

Then try this new **FollowLine** subroutine in place of the old one.

```
FollowLine:
  while True
    a=rSense()
    if a=2 or a= 3 or a=7 or a = 6
      rForward 1
    elseif a=1
      rTurn 2
      LT=1
    elseif a=4
      rTurn -2
      LT=-1
    elseif a=5 or a=0
      rTurn LT
    endif
  wend
return
```

This is not a perfect solution, but it is amusing. See if you can improve on it.

Solutions: Chapter 8

Solution for Exercise 8.2

Try this program

```
MainProgram:
  gosub Initialize
  Found=False
  repeat
    gosub RoamSome
    gosub LookForRed
  until Found
  xyString 10,580,"Found It"
end
//-----------------------------
Initialize:
  // create robot
  rLocate 50,50
  // make three objects
  rTurn -100-random(100)
  s=random(50)
  circle 200-s,300-s,400+s,350+s,Black,DarkGray
  s=random(50)
  rectangle 550-s,400-s,600+s,400+s,Black,DarkGray
  Line 300,100,600,200,50,DarkGray
  // create an object to find
  // choose from two places
  s=15
  if random(100)<50
    circle 700-s,100-s,700+s,100+s,RED,RED
  else
    circle 300-s,500-s,300+s,500+s,RED,RED
  endif
return
//-----------------------------
LookForRed:
  xyString 10,580,"Looking "
  for a=1 to 360
    rTurn 1
    if rLook()=Red then break
  next
  if rLook()=Red then gosub GoToIt
return
GoToIt:
  xyString 10,580,"Go to it"
  while rBumper()=0
```

```
     rForward 1
  wend
  if rBeacon(RED)>0 and rBeacon(RED)<15
    Found=true
  endif
return
//----------------------------
RoamSome:
   for i= 1 to 200
      if rBumper() = 0
         rForward 1
      else
         gosub TurnAway
      endif
   next
Return
//----------------------------
TurnAway:
   if rBumper()=4
      rTurn 150+random (61)
   elseif rBumper()=2
      rTurn -90-random(20)
   elseif rBumper()=8
      rTurn 90+random(20)
   elseif rBumper()=6
      rTurn -200-random(70)
   elseif rBumper()=12
      rTurn 200+random(70)
   endif
   rForward 1
Return
```

Solutions: Chapter 9

Solution for Exercise 9.1
Combine Figures 9.1 and 9.3. Remember that **MainProgram** always has to be the topmost.

Solution for Exercise 9.2
Replace the **RunMaze** subroutine from above with the two subroutines given in Figure 9.4.

Solution for Exercise 9.3
Add the code given in Figure 9.6 to the bottom of the **Initialization** subroutine from above. Then replace the **RunMaze** subroutine with the new one given in Figure 9.7.

Solution for Exercise 9.4
Change the line in the **RunMaze** subroutine from above that says
```
    for i=0 to 3
```
With
```
    for i=0 to 6
```

Then replace the code that was in Figure 9.6 that you added at the bottom of the **Initialization** subroutine with this code instead:
```
        Dim A[7]
        A[0]=90
        A[1]=90
        A[2]=-90
        A[3]=-90
        A[4]=90
        A[5]=90
        A[6]=180
```

Solution for Exercise 9.5

Right after the `rLocate` statement in the **Initialization** subroutine add `rSlip 5`. Also in the **ForwardTillBlocked** subroutine change `rFeel()` to `rDFeel(Red)`.

Solution for Exercise 9.6

Replace the **ForwardTillBlocked** subroutine from above with the one given in Figure 9.8. You may want to add these lines right after the `rSlip 5` line in the **Initialization** subroutine.

```
LineWidth 10
rInvisible Green
rPen Down
```

Solution for Exercise 9.7

This exercise is left up to you. However, here is an interesting exercise that combines the Line Following algorithms you have seen in Chapter 7 and the stuff you have here. (Think of Crumbs Trail!)

Remove the `rSlip 5` line you added above. Make sure you have added the lines that lowers the pen as shown above. Now add this line to the **MainProgram** right above the `End` statement: `Gosub FollowLine`

Now also add this **FollowLine** subroutine to your program and run it.

```
FollowLine:
  i = 0
  repeat
    a = rSense()
    if a <> 0
      rForward 1
    else
      rForward 17
      rTurn -A[i]
      i = i+1
    endif
  until i = 7
Return
```

Solutions: Chapter 10

Solution for Exercise 10.2

Here is a new **FindAngles** subroutine that uses arrays and a bit of math to achieve the same work but with shorter code (11 less lines). Notice that it is shorter but not as easy to read and understand. It may be better sometimes to have the longer code since other people can understand it and change it easier than the shorter but less understandable code.

```
FindAngles:
  dim Values[2,3]        //array to hold angles
  Values[0,0] = Red      //one row for Red
  Values[1,0] = Green    //and one row for green
  for j=1 to 2
    For i=0 to 1
      for a= 1 to 360
        if rBeacon(Values[i,0])
          A=90-rCompass()
          if A<0 then A=A+360
          Values[i,j] = A
          break
        endif
        rTurn 2*j-3 //-1 when j=1 and 1 when j=2
      next            //for clockwise then counter
    next
  next
  //average the angles in the two columns of each row
  Ar=(Values[0,1]+Values[0,2])/2
  Ag=(Values[1,1]+Values[1,2])/2
Return
```

Solutions: Chapter 11

The exercises in Chapter 11 are open ended small projects that should be interesting to tackle in the class room as group projects.

Solutions: Chapter 12

The exercises in Chapter 12 are open ended projects that should be interesting to tackle in the class room as group projects.

Index